WHAT KIND OF ANGRY PERSON ARE YOU?

Are you a stuffer—overeating, over-drinking, and smoking too much in order to swallow your rage?

Are you an actor—constantly telling people how angry you are, without doing anything about it?

Are you a body person—prey to mysterious aches and pains, chills and ills that no doctor can cure?

Are you an angry parent—teaching your children to be as frightened of their anger as you are of yours?

Or are you one of the many other types of people whose anger comes out in ways that they do not suspect but most certainly suffer from?

This book by a leading psychologist will show you how to face the anger within you without fear or guilt —and how to let it flow freely out of you through channels that will enrich rather than poison the quality of your life.

HOW TO GET ANGRY WITHOUT FEELING GUILTY

How to Get Angry Without Feeling Guilty

by ADELAIDE BRY

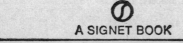

A SIGNET BOOK

NEW AMERICAN LIBRARY

SIGNET TRADEMARK REG. U.S. PAT. OFF. AND FOREIGN COUNTRIES
REGISTERED TRADEMARK–MARCA REGISTRADA
HECHO EN WINNIPEG, CANADA

SIGNET, SIGNET CLASSIC, MENTOR, ONYX, PLUME, MERIDIAN AND NAL
BOOKS are published by NAL Penguin Inc.,
1633 Broadway, New York, New York 10019

First Signet Printing, January, 1977

7   8   9   10   11   12   13   14   15

PRINTED IN CANADA

To George
in love and anger

My special thanks to so many people who shared their angry feelings and filled out an anger questionnaire. One is at the end of the book for you and your family and friends.

Special thanks to: Dr. Edward B. Guy, Melvin H. Heller, Peter Tauber, Sue Roberts, Margaret Danbrot, Michael Karp, Johanna Schlesinger, Prospect Hill, Conrad Sponholz, and the MacDowell Colony.

Table of Contents

This is a book about ANGER.

You have to begin at the beginning.

The beginning is admitting it.

Next is recognizing it, spotting it in yourself and others.

Then comes deciding what you are going to do about it.

Finally, the very last step is a feeling of vast relief.
    Guilt, tears, frustration, tensions will go away.

Now what?

Just accept and enjoy.

Until.

Until when?

Until the whole thing begins all over again.

WHAT ANGER MEANS IN THIS BOOK, IN YOU AND IN YOUR LIFE.

ANGER IS . . . ENERGY.

ANGER CAN . . . GIVE YOU STRENGTH.

ANGER CAN . . . DESTROY YOU AND OTHERS.

ANGER CAN RELEASE WARMTH AND GOOD FEELINGS AND GIVE YOU RELIEF FROM TENSION.

RIGHT NOW, THIS MOMENT, WHAT DOES ANGER DO FOR YOU?

Anger is by definition:
A strong feeling of displeasure and belligerence aroused by a real or supposed wrong.

Random House Dictionary of the English Language

What Anger Is All About

In these liberated times, men and women come into my office and in the most matter-of-fact way describe their sexual behavior. They talk about techniques, positions, partners. They tell me about their orgasms and their impotency, their fantasies and their infidelities.

But when the talk turns to anger, many of these same people clam up. Or else they squirm in their chairs, gaze off into space and speak haltingly, hesitating over every other word. Often, shame and embarrassment cloud the recounting of an angry incident. And some people tell me they "can't even remember" the last time they felt anger (they've pushed it so far down).

Sex and sexual feelings are okay now. Respectable, at least in the sense that most people can own up to what they do and don't do, feel and don't feel. But anger is the dirty word. The obscene topic. The unacceptable, unrespectable feeling.

Time and again, I've heard people deny or apologize for their anger, seeing it as an ugly personal blot, a shameful character defect that must be subdued, ignored, overcome, eradicated; or, as the evil and insidious emotion responsible for getting all of us, humankind and the world, into our present sorry state.

It seems we should have learned something from the recent turnabout in our collective attitude toward sex. Sexual feelings, we've decided—and not so very long ago at that—are not bad. Or harmful. Only sexual feelings that are repressed and twisted are.

In the same way, anger is not bad. It's an honest, forthright, decent emotion, a life-giving motivating force. But anger that is denied, distorted, and/or misused can be very harmful indeed. Unfortunately, too many people deny, distort, and misuse their anger.

As a therapist, I've seen how suppressed anger festers in the mind and body of the individual, creating both emotional and physical ailments; how it insinuates itself between husband and wife, and between friend and friend, dissolving all the good, warm feelings that first brought them together; how it poisons relationships at work, at school, at play, in love, in all of life itself.

Worst of all, I've seen the stage set for more of the same: I've seen parents, "modern" young mothers and fathers who wouldn't dream of squelching their kids' normal, healthy expressions of sexuality, deny their children's equally normal, healthy expressions of anger. (As in "You're not *really* angry at your brother for breaking the doll. After all, he's just a baby." Or "You don't care about me, you're angry at me." Or "Mustn't be angry at Mommy. It's not *nice*.") And so, a new generation grows up burdened with guilt and unresolved anger.

It's always fascinating to read some anthropologist's description of a happy, peaceful tribe way out in the middle of nowhere to whom anger is no problem because (incorporated into a kind of unwritten master plan) there are traditional, ritualized ways of dealing with it. It's interesting to speculate that this is how it _could_ be for us ... if only.

However, we're not living there, in that remote culture, but here, in this crowded, confused, quick-changing last quarter of the twentieth century. We have feelings and they must be dealt with and, lacking a master plan, we must each find our own best ways of handling them.

That's what this book is all about—new ways of thinking about anger, new ways of exercising it. controlling it, expressing and truly accepting it.

Honest anger appropriately expressed can help you get more of what you want out of life.

It can make you feel better about yourself.

It can make all your relationships more meaningful and _real_.

It can help relieve both physical and emotional stress.

It can whet your sexual appetite.

But before any of this can happen, anger must be confronted and examined. It must be looked at and accepted for what it is: a powerful primary emotion that, like all other emotions, is positive or negative, bad or good, constructive or destructive, according to what you do with it.

There are more ways of expressing anger than you might ever have thought possible, and my one directive, as you begin to read the following pages is to say to yourself, "It's perfectly okay for me to get mad, it won't drive my loved ones away and I don't have to feel guilty." Learn to totally accept anger and realize how it can work for you.

Once Upon a Time

In my family, they slammed bedroom doors, shouted, cried, sulked, and withdrew. Sometimes someone got slapped or spanked. I was ashamed of us and the way we acted toward one another. I was sure we weren't like other families and I shuddered to think that some day everyone, friends at school, the neighbors, would find out what terrible, bad people we were.

Well, we weren't bad, of course. And as for being different, we weren't that, either. We were an ordinary, everyday family: a mother, a father, and three children, each of us locked into his or her own pathetically ineffective way of dealing with an emotion we neither understood nor called by its rightful name: anger.

Now I know that when my sister cried herself to sleep, she was crying in anger.

That when my brother locked himself in his room and didn't reappear for hours, he was withdrawing because he had no other way of handling his angry feelings.

That when my mother flew into a tantrum (yes, grown-ups have temper tantrums, too), it was because of the anger—the *rage*—she felt at having no suitable outlet for her considerable talents and energies.

That my father's "weak stomach," which made it necessary for him to periodically visit some clinic or other for tests, rest, and special dietary recommendations, was the result of unresolved anger.

It took me years to understand that a friend who was always late was expressing her anger; that a housekeeper of mine, a woman who frequently broke dishes and glassware and damaged several small, inexpensive, but nevertheless precious-to-me bibelots (and who always profusely apologized for these "accidents") was also telegraphing angry feelings; that a male acquaintance, known for his jokes and witty, often barbed remarks was using his sense of humor as a shield to protect himself from his own anger and everyone else's.

As for me, I realize now that during all my growing-up years, and for many years thereafter, my way of dealing with anger was to put on a happy face and pretend it didn't exist. To the world at large I was an easygoing, undemanding, seemingly always happy young woman who never uttered a sharp or unkind word. Mostly, I believed that this gracious, sunnyside-up personality I'd assumed was the real me.

Occasionally, though, some of the anger burst through, and when it did, I felt guilty, worthless, out of control. I hated my anger and turned it back upon myself.

When my children got out of hand and I took a swat at them, or when they had problems and seemed unhappy, I became angry. But not at them—at me, for being a bad mother. When I realized that my marriage was falling apart, I was angry at *me* because it seemed that *I* had failed.

You see, though I grew up with many "advantages"—I went to good schools, was taught to dance, swim, and ride horseback, had music and art lessons, and was taken to plays and museums—I never learned anything about anger except what I absorbed, through my very pores, as a child: that it was dangerous and bad, a second-rate emotion for second-rate people.

Sure, I reasoned, little kids could occasionally succumb to anger, and lesser people who didn't know any better . . . the failures, the small-minded, the undisciplined. But successful, worthwhile, good people? No. I was convinced that anger had no place in their repertoire of emotions.

Now, of course, I know what utter nonsense this idea is. We're *all* angry some of the time. We all go through life with a bag of anger slung over one shoulder.

There's nothing shameful about that bag of anger, either. It has a purpose. Later on we'll explore ways of opening it up, examining its contents, learning how to make good use of what is inside. But first, let's consider how it got there.

Once upon a time, you were a little baby. You had needs, things that were necessary to your very survival.

Food was one of them, and warmth, and closeness to other human beings. Some of the time these needs were satisfied without your even having to ask: you were fed before you were aware of your hunger, changed before you sensed the cold wetness of your diaper, sung to and rocked before loneliness had a chance to take hold.

Other times you had to wait for attention. You became hungry or cold. You didn't like these feelings and you signaled your distress by crying. If your cries were ignored, or if your parents were slow to answer, you felt frustrated and your cries took on a louder, lustier tone. These were your first experiences with anger.

If your parents loved you and were reasonably concerned, they did come, sooner or later, and gave you warm milk, wiped your rear end, cuddled you, talked to you, lulled you back to sleep. Anger got you what you wanted. It was resolved and soon forgotten.

Then, paradise lost. You got bigger and life became more complicated. You had the same needs, but the instances of their direct, immediate gratification became fewer and farther between as your parents, anxious for you to learn new behaviors, began to make demands. They wanted you to drink from a glass (and give up that nice, warm nipple) ; sit up in a high chair (instead of being held close in loving arms) ; and later on, use the toilet (outrageous! the end of spontaneity, or so it must have seemed) . In other words, you were systematically frustrated.

The growing-up process, by which we become self-controlled and self-sustaining adults, is always an exercise in frustration. As Leo Madow puts it in his book *Anger,* "The child goes from being nursed and completely cared for to eating and drinking from plates and cups, to eating at set times, postponing the gratification of hunger until a set meal time, and eventually reaches the stage when he must earn the money to buy the food before he can have it. All this leads to anger and resentment, usually unrecognized."

So, you, I, all of us, acquired our personal bags of anger very early on in life. As to why one person's bag is heavier than another's, the difference has to do with our individual psychological makeups plus the circumstances under which we grew.

For some infants, those whose basic needs for food, warmth, and love are not satisfactorily met, there is such frustration that it seems obvious why their anger accumulates early and strong. A few theorists go back even further, to the very beginning, and believe that even the way one is brought into the world may have some effect on one's anger quotient.

French obstetrician Frederick Leboyer, for example, is convinced that what happens at the time of birth may influence the individual's future emotional well-being. Instead of the abrupt, traumatic exit from the womb into the harshly lit noise and confusion of the ordinary modern-day hospital delivery room, the hasty snipping of the umbilical cord (which Leboyer is quoted as calling "an act of the greatest cruelty, whose negative effect one can hardly measure"), and the sharp smack on the behind, with which so many infants are delivered, Leboyer eases the baby's way from womb to world. The delivery area is kept semi-dark, shadowy, and silent. The newborn is placed on its mother's stomach, umbilical cord intact, and lovingly massaged for five minutes or so, after which the cord is severed and the baby is placed tenderly into a small tub of warm water. In his book *Birth Without Violence*, Leboyer says: "What might have remained of fear, stiffness, tension now melts away like snow in the sunshine. Everything in the baby's body which was still anxious, rigid and blocked starts to live, to dance."

Leboyer has been using this method for only about five years now. Dr. Danielle Rapoport of the Sorbonne did a follow-up study of fifty of the children he delivered. In *The New York Times* she is quoted as saying, among other things, "The children I have studied have been spared nearly all of the major and minor psychopathologies—of eating, sleeping, maternal relations, etc.—of infancy." Whether they will continue to be "noticeably different" (as Dr. Rapoport puts it) from other children, delivered in the usual way, remains to be seen. It does seem likely, to me at any rate, that the birth trauma may be more significant than we have previously suspected and that the ease, or dis-ease, with which we are brought into the world may have life-long repercussions in terms of muscular tension rooted in the body during the first moments of life. It will be interesting to know what becomes of these children, to follow their emotional development, to discover what they, with their gentle ushering into the world, do with *their* angers and frustrations.

No two children, not even twins, ever get exactly the same treatment from their mother and father. Parents react differently to each child, and this in turn influences the child's own emotional development, and thus has some bearing on how much (or how little) anger one feels and what one does with it in adulthood. The order of birth—whether a child is the first-, second-, third-born, in the family—is particularly significant.

If you were a first child, for example, you experienced anger at the arrival of a younger sibling. Each child wants to be the only child, and when the new arrival comes, one's whole world is changed. But parents are reluctant to accept the fact of sibling rivalry and the continuous stream of angry feelings an older "displaced" child has toward a younger one. They may react with shocked disbelief or anger when they perceive the first child does not immediately respond with warmth and love to the younger one although the feelings are perfectly natural. It's the action the older child could take that bears watching—not the normal emotions.

How the parents handle the situation, the degree of acceptance or rejection of the older child's feelings begins to determine the degree of anger "built-into" the child. It is never easy. The child gets the idea that he's "supposed" to feel one way (love the new arrival), but, in fact, he feels just the opposite. He may even begin to doubt his own feelings.

This split between what is actually *felt*, and the way one feels compelled to *act* in order to retain the parents' love and protection is what hurts and confuses. The small child, whose very being is threatened by loss of love, will do anything to keep it—even put away his honest feelings of anger.

The child is in a bind. He must depend on his parents for food and shelter and, just as important, for love, and so he must do all he can to stay "lovable" (otherwise, they might abandon him). No other species has such a long dependency period; the child is helpless for years and years, and this, of course, contributes to the depth of the problem.

At some point in childhood, sexual rivalry adds a whole new dimension to young angry feelings. The little girl becomes angry at her mother because Daddy belongs to Mommy and not to her (or at least not in *that* way). But—more conflict and confusion—how *can* one be angry at one's own dear Mommy when she loves you so, and you after all love her too? Boys experience the same kind of anger toward their fathers and react to their feelings with similar guilt and confusion.

Some people work through these particular feelings; others don't, with the result that some bags of anger get very heavy. And something else begins to happen. The child becomes rutted into a single way of handling anger. He or she keeps doing "it" over and over again—denying, blaming, sulking, having tantrums, depending on what is tolerated in the family. A lifetime pattern begins to emerge.

As he grows older, the child meets with more frustration which generates more and more anger. Maybe he doesn't like his looks (he's "too short," "too tall," "too fat," "too thin," "too light," "too dark," "too something"). But there's little he can do about it. Or maybe he thinks he isn't bright enough (or resents being thought of as "a brain"). Or not athletic enough. Or not popular. Maybe he has trouble making friends, getting good grades, attracting members of the opposite sex. The inevitable result is frustration, which leads to anger, sometimes directed at himself, sometimes at other people (parents, teachers, the kids at school, sisters and brothers), sometimes at circumstances and events over which he feels he has no control.

At the moment of falling in love, one temporarily suppresses the anger, because the joys of sex and mutual self-discovery are so gratifying. But later on, when some of the newness wears off, the anger emerges again, and therein lies one problem in male-female relationships. That anger was there all the time, right from the beginning, but the mating urge is so strong one simply puts a temporary lid on it.

When the young adult finds someone with whom to spend "the rest of his life," he's expected to settle down, earn a living, raise children. Maybe he welcomes his new responsibilities, maybe not. In any case, marriage usually carries with it some frustration, which leads to anger. Inflation eats into the paycheck. Someone else gets the big promotion at work. The new car is a lemon. The neighbor's dog digs up the tulip bulbs . . . and . . . well, you get the picture.

The point, of course, is that we all go through life experiencing some frustration at every step, or at least every other step along the way. And frustration is the parent of anger.

Frustration isn't all bad. The "right" amount of it is the energizer that helps us overcome our difficulties, the motivating force that spurs us on to achievement and success. Ideally, we would all grow up under conditions that made us feel loved and frustrated "just enough." But unfortunately, no one has ever determined just how much is "just enough," let alone figured out how to prescribe so that each growing child gets the proper dose—neither too much nor too little of the stuff.

Very few people are lucky enough to receive that perfect balance of love and just enough frustration. Many of us are overdosed with frustration which is not too harmful in itself—IF we can handle the natural by-product of frustration: anger. When anger is successfully managed and processed, when the individual can recognize his anger and then do something to relieve it, his bag of anger won't weigh too heavily. It doesn't prevent him from living fully and well; indeed, it is often *useful*. It helps him get some of the things he wants out of life. But if he mismanages his anger, if he can't (or won't) recognize the feeling and/or handles it in self-destructive ways, his bag of anger becomes debilitating; it immobilizes him as effectively as a two-ton lead weight strapped to one leg.

The mind is an amazing recorder of events and feelings. Every single thing that ever happened to you is there, somewhere in your memory. In a sense, you have a whole personal history book up there inside your head. But because of the way the mind works, it's a strange kind of text. The chronology may be wrong, and over the years much of what "really happened" gets censored. The mind puts some pages up front and completely blacks out others; one's conscious life is merely a few thin chapters, while the bulk of the book lies buried underneath.

Yet your total way of being in the world, the "vibes" you radiate to others, your laughter, warmth, sadness, despair, depression, and yes, anger, all of these make up the total book of you whether or not your behavior is consciously expressive of them. Think for a moment of someone you've met recently. Didn't you get a total impression—not just of features, body, clothes, age, etc.? Wasn't there something more? A kind of radiance, an aura of personality? One person's aura encourages you to come closer ("I want to know him/her better," you say to yourself), while another's, for some reason you can't quite "put your finger on," sends you running.

Your own aura, made up of all your feelings and perceptions, began to coalesce long, long ago. And, of course, your anger was part of it. What you learned as a child about anger; what you expressed or did not express; what you saw in your family every day; what your brothers and sisters and playmates did with *their* anger—all of this is an integral part of your *total* history.

One of the purposes of this book is to help you to trigger your memories of anger, to help you understand what you learned when you were little which still may play a part in your life to this very day; to let you know that if you are indeed willing to open yourself to new feelings and new behavior, you can expand your *whole* range of being. Focusing on anger may trigger other releases in mind and body, may liberate the good feelings that till now were deeply buried. Once you open up any part of yourself that was previously locked up tight, little by little other parts, too, begin to emerge. You become more fully human.

If you can find within yourself a place for your anger, if you can say to yourself, "It's okay, because it's part of me," and if you can at the same time respect the anger rights of others (especially your children), then you are taking a step toward wholeness and you are also truly expressing love. Because what love is, I think, is letting be. Letting yourself be what you wholly are. And letting others be totally themselves too.

Directing as a way of life—doing, being, feeling what you think you *should*, rather than what you *are*—is ultimately unsatisfactory. Directing yourself invalidates your own authenticity. Directing others invalidates theirs. Denying or trying to change any emotion, whether it be love or hate or anger, involves a tremendous expenditure of psychic energy which is always better spent otherwise.

Feelings don't go away just because you deny them.

Anger, especially, just stays there, festering unless you bring it up for light and air. Once out in the open, it's always far less threatening both to you and your feelings about yourself, and to your relationships with others. You can look at it, treat it as the vital part of yourself that it is, decide what to do with it. In short, it will fit quite naturally into its proper place within the wide range of human emotions, to be called upon and experienced like any other. And, in the process, the whole of you will be expanded.

New Ways with Old Anger

Anger

As you see the word "anger" printed here, what pops into your mind? Fear? Punishment? Mother? Father? A locked room? A headache? Sex? Whatever the image or words, I'd be willing to bet that your associations with anger go a long way back to when you were small, and that the way you deal with your anger right now, today, is but a more sophisticated grown-up version of what you did with it when you were a little boy or girl. But there are more ways of feeling and behaving than what you learned in one home, from one mother and father. Yes, there's lots more to it than that.

We all get angry at least occasionally, and some of us are angry almost all of the time. Maybe you feel anger but you don't know what to do about it (because you never learned). Maybe you feel it and you always end up doing the same inappropriate or self-destructive thing (because it's what you learned). Or maybe you've trained yourself not to feel it, with a vague awareness that something—what could it be?—just isn't right. (Again, because of what you learned.)

What can you do about it?

You can begin to relearn how to think and feel and express your anger. But first you have to give yourself permission to become a whole, healthy individual who not only feels the emotion but accepts it. And to do this, you may have to clear your head of some of the following ideas about anger:

That expressing it directly is childish and bad.

That crying is never done out of anger, but only out of sadness.

That crying is unmanly (or immature).

That losing your temper is a terrible thing.

That control is everything.

That people who have tantrums are sick.

That hot-headed people are not to be trusted.

That to stay calm and smiling is the ultimate goal.

That when a child says to a parent, "I wish you were dead," he is a "bad" child.

That when a grown-up thinks to himself, "I wish he (or she) were dead," he is a "bad" grown-up.

That anger is not worthy of you.

Anger is worthy of you because it's part of you. It's a good, honest emotion that can help you get more of what you want out of life. Angry feelings tell you that something is not the way you'd like it to be. They are your signal to *do* something. Anger energizes. You can use it to write a book, play golf, enjoy sex, get to be the president of the company . . . or, it can give you ulcers, a backache, cause you to become depressed, hate life, sit in a corner and destroy yourself with liquor or drugs or overeating.

This book is about learning to make choices as to how that energy—that anger—can be used to best advantage, in a way that doesn't jeopardize good feelings about yourself or the feelings that flow between you and others you care about.

You can't begin to make choices about what to do with your anger, however, until you know for sure that you *are* angry. Strangely enough, the emotion which comes through loud and unmistakably clear to some people is very difficult for others to identify. Perhaps you're one of the latter. Perhaps you're often aware of a feeling of discomfort or uneasiness that is hard to classify. "Anger" may seem too strong a word. Or perhaps you associate anger with "rage" and what *you're* feeling is not so much red-hot as blue. Reconsider. Anger goes under many guises. Consider the following phrases, for example:

I'm fed up.
I've had it.
I'm disappointed.
I'm down in the dumps.
My feelings are hurt.
I'm sad.
I'm hungry.
Who needs it?
I have a headache.
I wish I could get away from it all.
What's the use?
I can't stand it!
What's the matter with her?
You give me a pain.
You make me laugh.

Whenever you say any of these things—or when you have the feeling that goes along with one of the phrases—suspect that you're angry. Because you possibly are.

When you're depressed, ask yourself what you're

angry about. You may not come up with an answer immediately, but look for one anyway.

When you say to yourself, "I feel sad (fed up, annoyed, hurt, disappointed) remember that these are simply anger words in disguise. Again, ask yourself what you're angry about.

Admit to yourself that when you are disappointed, you're also likely to be angry; when your feelings are hurt, underneath it all you're angry at the person who did the hurting; when you're frustrated, even though you keep a stiff upper lip and don't make a big deal about it, you are really and truly very angry.

Also, remember that anger is not necessarily reasonable or justifiable, any more than love is. Emotions are rarely logical or objective, and just as we're all capable of loving unwisely, of giving ourselves to someone who, objectively, is unworthy of our affections, we all may feel anger when, again objectively, it "doesn't make sense." A good example is the anger we feel when the car breaks down. We know that the car, an inanimate object, didn't break down on purpose, its intentions were not malicious. Yet who can deny feeling angry at a car that leaves us stranded in the middle of nowhere, and which will cost us goodness only knows how many dollars to repair? It's the same with people, only we're much more inclined to deny our anger when logic tells us that the person who hurt or inconvenienced us did so unaware and with no evil intent. Excuse the person, if you must, but acknowledge your anger. To do otherwise is to be unnecessarily hard on yourself.

Why would you want to deny your anger anyway? Well, if you grew up in a home where anger was considered bad, dirty, evil, and unbecoming to a child—and since many of us did come out of such environments—you got the message. And since you didn't want to be considered bad, dirty, or evil, you simply avoided expressing the way you felt in a direct way and learned to disguise your emotions instead. Some people, and perhaps you're one of them, become so good at pretending they're not angry that they manage to fool even themselves.

If you're ambiguous about anger, right now ask yourself whether you ever feel the emotion. First, try to remember having real, righteous, up-front anger, which is usually a response to some kind of threat either to you or a member of your family, or to a cherished belief or ideal. (Do you know that feeling? Have you had it and done something—anything—about it? Have you had it and hid it?)

Now, there's another kind of anger. This is the old anger that hides behind other feelings: depression, for example; sadness; guilt. Almost always, when you're feeling one of these other emotions, there's old anger from the past lurking just below the surface. (Have you ever been aware of disguised anger? Have you been able to uncover it? If so, what did you do about it?)

Okay, so we have two kinds of anger. The first comes as a response to an immediate threat: let's say a bully is picking on your child. Enraged, you run out, screaming at the bully, and chase him away. Your anger is justified, your response appropriate. You may re-experience the anger each time you think about the incident, but the feeling isn't festering in your gut.

The other old, disguised angers aren't so easy.

People spend years in therapy learning first to recognize them and then how to deal with them. Usually this is a process of coming to understand that what happened in the past, with Mommy and Daddy, is not the same as what is happening now. Once you can grasp this, you can shake yourself free of the past and rid yourself of those disguised angers, the result of deeply embedded frustrations from your childhood.

It isn't easy. Just knowing that anger is there, calling it by its real name, is a start. But the effort must also be made to identify those disguised angers, feel them, deal with them as though they were real. Because they are real. Many of the anger exercises in this book are designed to help you get to the source of those old, disguised angers. They've worked for many people and I want you to give them a try.

Getting to the source of those old, disguised angers is a goal well worth working toward, but dealing with your anger in the here and now is, I feel, equally important.

A good way to begin is to define your own feelings about the emotion. In the process of writing this book, I invited more than a hundred people to complete an anger questionnaire. One of the items on the questionnaire involved completing a sentence which began:

Anger is _____ (fill in whatever pops into your mind).

The results were enormously interesting, both to me and, more important, to the respondents themselves. So for a start, I suggest that you, too, sit down and complete the "Anger is _____" statement.

Many of the respondents told me that they had

never thought so specifically about their own anger before, nor had they ever come to such close grips with their feelings about the emotion. Several expressed curiosity about what the other respondents had written, and when I showed them (the questionnaires were unsigned), they were amazed by the variety of answers.

Here is a sampling of the response from the "Anger is _____" item.

ANGER IS

... sometimes justified, but an indication of maladjustment when expressed too frequently.
... hating authority figures.
... a general feeling of resentment, shown in words.
... venting your feelings.
... something I try to control.
... an excellent way of making your point.
... an emotion to express feelings of frustration at myself.
... a scary and difficult emotion; its expression is followed by punishment and isolation for me.
... a response to threats of nonexistence.
... a self-directed response to frustration.
... sometimes productive, more often destructive.
... a feeling hard for me to express.
... a wasted emotion.
... an expression that makes other people reject me.
... a healthy emotion.
... a means of releasing internal pressure.

... an unpleasant, bad feeling.

... a safety valve.

... a gut response to something you don't like.

... inability to cope with life.

... yelling and screaming.

... a desire to destroy the other person.

... my internalized response to threat, real or make-believe.

... not liking yourself more than you dislike the person who makes you angry.

You might find you're better able to think through your own feelings about anger in general if you make the effort to put them all down on paper, and for this reason I'm including a blank anger questionnaire, essentially the same as the ones I used as background for writing this book. (Assuming that you, too, are curious about how others feel about anger, I'm also including an example of one of the over 100 completed questionnaires. You'll find it on page 171).

To begin, go through the following chapters and read about the many different ways people handle their anger. Then see if you can identify your own ways of dealing with the emotion. At the same time, try to understand that while anger itself is never bad, there are some modes of expression that are unacceptable such as those which are self-destructive to you either emotionally or physically, and those which are destructive to others. However, within a large range, there are various acceptable and appropriate ways to express your anger, and it's within your power to choose what is ultimately best for you.

Sometimes (but not always), confronting your boss on an important issue is best.

Sometimes, playing a fast game of tennis is the answer.

Sometimes, telling your spouse you're really angry is right.

Sometimes, holding your tongue and listening to his/her anger is more appropriate.

Occasionally, banging your fist on the table may give you immediate relief. Or slamming the door, walking outside and breathing some good fresh air.

Sitting down and writing out your feelings is another way.

Making a joke often clears the air of tension.

Or deep breathing exercises. Or yoga.

Or having a temper tantrum.

How will you know what to do and when to do it? Only by practice and by thinking through what you learned when you were little and then deciding for yourself what's best for the moment.

No one way is best all the time. No one way is best for everyone.

As you learn to work with your anger, you will find you're also working with yourself. As you accept your anger, you accept yourself. As you accept yourself, you'll understand others; and just beyond understanding is love.

Spotting Your Type of Anger

Each of the following chapters describes the different ways in which people deal with anger, and you are now going to discover which type or combination of types, if you have more than one way of expressing it, you are.

The order of these angers is alphabetical; there is no preference, no one is "better" than any other.

ACTOR
BIG TALKER
BLAMER
BODY PERSON
COMEDIAN
CORNER PERSON
CREATOR
DAYDREAMER
DOER
SABOTEUR
SEXED-UP ANGRY COUPLE
STUFFER

The Actor

"When I get angry, I want to *punch*. When I was a kid, I punched other kids in the neighborhood. Now I bang my fist down hard . . ."

An Actor

"When I get angry, I have to *do* something. Yes, I'm ashamed to say that I throw things sometimes. But I'm careful when I throw—nothing breakable, and I aim so I don't hit anyone."

Another Actor

"I love a good cry . . ."

A Third Actor

The actor creates scenes, uses his or her body to *dramatize* anger.

Who hasn't watched a toddler, down on the floor, face red, screaming at the top of his lungs, legs kicking, body writhing, letting the whole world know, in no uncertain terms, that things are not going just exactly the way he or she wants them to?

And then there is the hitting, biting, hair-pulling, and spitting of the small child. Here again, we have the miniature master Actor expressing rage.

One six-year-old I know managed to topple a bookcase, and something like three hundred paperbacks came tumbling down onto the floor. The child looked with positive awe and amazement mixed with pleasure at what she'd done.

In expressing anger with a vengeance, the Actor feels, like this little girl, a sense of accomplishment. Something has been *done*. Even though that something might have been destructive, the act itself brings a sense of relief. Tension has been dissipated.

The older Actor, no longer five, but a grownup, "mature" adult—what does he do with the anger-of-the-body that still lives within him?

One brilliant young man I know, home on vacation from a large eastern university, became so angry at his mother that he put his fist through a plaster wall!

Another Actor, a woman in her forties who had finally decided to leave her husband after twenty-eight years of marriage, heaved a giant television set from its stand onto the floor. "Afterward, I couldn't help laughing," she told me. "The set landed on its side, but it kept right on playing. That inane talk-show chatter kept right on going. It was like my marriage, my husband. Our relationship was collapsing, but he went right along, business as usual, as though nothing was happening. Just like that set."

More restrained Actors play their scenes with less flamboyance. Crying, slamming a door, pounding on a table, brandishing a clenched fist, throwing small objects (a pencil, a toothbrush) or unbreakables (pillows, shoes) afford them the physical release that dissipates anger, makes it vanish like clouds dispersing after a thunderstorm.

Since children tend to take their anger cues from their parents, the child who grows up in a home where physically aggressive expressions of anger are common, where one or both parents hurled objects, or verbal abuse, slammed doors, pounded fists down on tables, etc., sees nothing unusual in these histrionics and, unless he was exposed to other, stronger influences, can be expected to model his behavior on theirs and become an Actor himself.

Or, the Actor might have discovered as a child that a temper tantrum can be a very effective tool indeed. Often, parents of Actors are cowed and back off when their children begin a tantrum. They (the parents) can't handle the scene, and they'll do *anything*, including giving in, to keep the peace and shut up their kids. The children learn soon enough that if being "reasonable" doesn't get them what they want, acting up probably will.

By adulthood, some Actors have modified and refined the techniques they had such success with as children. But acting is still instrumental in getting them what they want. Imagine an executive chairing a board meeting—the kind of man who gets red in the face when challenged or opposed— he pounds the table and gets his points across by shouting, grimacing, stabbing his finger in the air. Often, businessmen of this type are despised by their subordinates, but they manage to keep tight control of the group while getting their own way.

This is because so many other people (non-Actors) are astonished and, yes, frightened when confronted by open and obvious expressions of anger. They don't know how far, nor to what lengths the angry one will go in order to get his own way; better to give in to the Actor rather than find out. Or so it seems.

Interestingly enough, however, the Actor is not always a *very* angry person and may, in fact, be far less angry than the outwardly smiling, inwardly seething, sulking person. Actors are simply very quick to display and *dramatize* their feelings.

(Obviously, there are exceptions: I'm thinking now of those few unfortunate people in our society who stagger under the weight of an intolerably large and impossible-to-manage bag of anger, the ones who express their anger by destroying property and by doing actual physical violence to themselves and to others. But these are not normal, ordinary, everyday Actors; they are severely disturbed people and should be recognized and treated as such.)

Are You an Actor?

Do you think of yourself (or have you heard yourself described) as being "quick-tempered" or "hot-headed?" When angry feelings well up within you, is your first impulse to *do* something (like cry? shout? throw? pound?) ? And do you often follow through on that impulse? If your answers are mostly "yes," you're probably an Actor.

Unlike other anger-types, many Actors feel quite comfortable with their way of handling anger. As one Actor put it: "Sure, I go on a little rampage now and then, do a little shouting, break a dish. But I never hurt anyone. And I'm not like some people I know. I don't hold a grudge. I don't stay mad for long. When I'm finished being angry, I'm finished. Biff, bang, it's over and done with."

Other Actors have more ambivalent feelings. They regret the momentary loss of control, wish they hadn't acted so "childishly," feel guilty and worry about having frightened or hurt the feelings of the person at whom their anger was directed. Sometimes, an Actor pays dearly for over-dramatizing. (A young husband, a nature-lover and self-admitted "ecology freak," got so angry at his wife that he ran outside, grabbed an ax, and chopped down one of the very young trees they had both lovingly planted a year or so previously. He sobbed uncontrollably as he told me the story. Another Actor, a woman, lost her temper and shouted at her boss; three days later she was fired.)

Assuming you are an Actor, how do *you* feel about your way of dealing with anger?

Perhaps you're one of those who feel satisfied, comfortable about it. If so, fine. Don't give up acting. Do keep in mind, however, that your dramatic outbursts may have an unsettling effect on others.

Be aware that while *you* may feel a sense of relief after one of your scenes because you've been able to get the anger out of *your* system, the person at whom your anger was directed may, unless he or she is also an Actor, continue to seethe. Many Actors are puzzled when this happens. *Their* anger is dissipated, but the other person's angry feelings linger on and may even be intensified by the Actor's blithe way of forgetting the incident.

Also, be aware that your scenes *do* tend to frighten certain kinds of people. Since your major concern should be *you*, not them, it would be reasonable for you to respond to this by saying, "Well, if I scare others, that's *their* problem."

Again, fine. The point, however, is that you understand how others might react and recognize the possibility that they will either shy away from you in the future, or that your scene has only heightened their anger, or that they may hold a grudge and try to get even.

If you are an Actor who has ruined a relationship, gotten so carried away with your scenes (like the young nature-lover who chopped down the sapling), and then regret your actions afterward, what can you do about it?

It's doubtful that you can, or even that you

should, give up acting. It's as valid a way of dealing with anger as any. But it's only *one* of *many* ways, and if always being the Actor leaves you feeling guilty, or your outbursts frighten you and/or others, explore alternate ways of expressing your feelings.

First, remember way back when you probably discovered that tantrums got good results with the grown-ups in your life. This is one reason why you continue to have those "tantrums."

Another reason is your adult joy of destruction. Most of us recognize that children get pleasure from destroying things. Who, in fact, doesn't remember working for hours building an elaborate sand castle and then spending a few glorious, exhilarating moments stomping it to ruins? Destruction, like creation, is accomplishment. As grown-ups, we like to think we've grown past the joy of destruction. But have we really? If so, why do those crowds gather to watch the demolition of an office building? Why did mobs gather to witness public executions?

Little children, who have no actual power or influence in the "real," adult world, have their tantrums and glory in the destruction they create. But, unless they happen to get hold of a loaded gun, only rarely does anyone get hurt by them.

As a grown-up Actor, understand that while you may gain some satisfaction from behavior you learned as a child, you don't *need* to resort to it because you're now a powerful adult and, unlike a five-year-old, you are strong and have options. Also, accept the fact that there will be times when no matter how you rant and rave, no matter what you destroy, you still won't be able to have things your way (a concept children have enormous trouble with).

Children, of course, have some anger outlets we adults don't; they can *play* out their anger in Mommy-and-Daddy games, cops-and-robbers, cowboys-and-Indians. Very often, the unwritten script for these games calls for someone to be severely punished, if not actually shot and killed. These fantasies—but remember it's serious business to the children playing them out—afford release for an accumulation of anger.

Here are a few ways in which you can constructively release your anger.

1. The next time you feel the impulse to chew someone out, do it. But do it in private, alone, in a room with the door closed. Better still, do it in front of a mirror, and get your act down on tape if you have a recording machine. Concentrate on making this one of the best performances of your life. Use your angriest, ugliest language to express just how you feel about what's bugging you. Put your whole body into it. Growl, snarl, grimace, posture, stamp your feet, wave your arms. Let it *all* out.

2. Buy a package of pencils and carry them with you in your pocket or purse. Next time you're angry enough to feel like destroying something, take out the pencils and one by one break them into pieces. (I've chosen pencils because they're portable, cheap, and make a highly satisfying "snap" as they are broken.)

3. Next time you feel like punching something, punch pillows. Or see if you can locate or make one of these special soft, down-filled

bats (about the size of a baseball bat, only much thicker) similar to the ones encounter group participants clobber each other with. Use it to attack the floor, the walls, the couch, your bed, anything solid, unyielding, and unbreakable.

4. Hammering, sawing, sculpting, target shooting are all good Actor activities that allow you the harmless physical release you seek. When an anger-provoking incident occurs, stuff your feelings for the moment. (This may not be easy, but your stuffing ability will increase with practice. And don't worry about becoming a chronic Stuffer; you are stuffing by *choice*, not because you must.) Then, when you have the time for it, let off steam with the appropriate activity.

5. Rediscover how to cry. Heavy sobbing and hysterical crying served you well as a child. Long, drawn-out tearful sessions in a darkened bedroom can give you the same release as more aggressive physical action, but with none of the destructive potential.

6. But most constructive of all, analyze your anger. In a moment of calm, think back over the last three or four times you played the Actor in an angry situation. Try to reconstruct each situation, one at a time. As you do so, ask yourself whether or not you feel good about the way you handled the incident. What makes these cases where you feel that acting was a good way of expressing your anger different from the ones in which you're sorry you created a scene? Can you recognize a pattern? If you could live through each incident again, what would you do? Now, anticipate a

similar or related incident and imagine yourself dealing with it. Imagine what would happen and how you would feel if you stuffed your anger. Made a joke. Talked it out calmly. Cried. Retreated. Went outside and ran three times around the block. Played tennis. Did twenty minutes of intense sitting-up exercises.

The Big Talker

"When I'm angry, I have this urge to tell it like it is ... and I usually do."

A Big Talker

"Sometimes the most abominable things pop out of my mouth. It's almost as though I'm not even aware of being angry until I've said something awful about somebody."

Another Big Talker

"My thing is, I can't stop putting myself down ... I can't stop telling the world what a stupid, incompetent, mean, angry dope I am."

A Third Big Talker

Talking it out is one of the best, healthiest, and most often-recommended ways of dealing with anger. Talking it out can clear the air, get our feelings across, and help us to understand one another better.

But there are good ways to talk it out, and there are other, self-defeating and unproductive ways.

Debbie is an example of a Big Talker. A pretty

young woman, Debbie has several rather disconcerting nervous mannerisms. She scratches her head a lot, chews her fingernails, bites her lower lip. At twenty-five, with her long, light-brown hair and boyish figure, she looks like a teen-ager. But she is already the mother of three toddlers. The children arrived at yearly intervals. The oldest is four.

Debbie is always quick to talk about how she feels, which is very often "angry." At the slightest prompting, she'll tell you, or anyone else who cares to listen, about how angry she was when her husband came home late last night, or when the supermarket clerk overcharged her three days ago, or when she discovered that a close friend had been talking about her behind her back. She "lets fly" (her words) at anything and anyone. No one is immune from her tongue-lashings, and she seems to be rather proud of the fact.

"I know if I can just get it off my chest, I'll feel better," Debbie told me. "Why, just the other day, the plumber came to put in the new dishwasher and he left the kitchen an absolute mess. Wrecked it, that's what he did. Just before he left, I gave him a piece of my mind. Told him off, but good. 'This is no way to behave in someone else's house,' I said. 'You're getting paid good money for this job, and you ought to have some consideration and clean up after yourself.' He started to interrupt, but I shut him up. 'Bet you don't go around leaving messes in your own house. So why do you come into mine and leave it looking like a cyclone hit it?' "

"Then when Bob [her husband] came home, I started to tell him about the plumber. Well, he walked out of the room right in the middle of the story. Now that's what I call *rude*. I followed him into the den and told him I thought his manners could use some improving. He just shook his head and turned on the TV. We just don't communicate anymore."

Big Talkers like Debbie have a lot in common with the Actor. But while the Actor relies mainly on body language to discharge his anger, the Big Talker gets immediate physical and emotional release through verbal explosions. Big Talkers, Actors, and other Doers tend to be a rather healthy lot. They're not usually susceptible to anger-induced psychosomatic ailments because they never allow angry feelings to accumulate. Instead, they "process" their anger as it arises, moving it up and out through their bodies, or, in the Big Talkers' case, through their mouths.

Big Talkers say what they feel, when they feel it, often regardless of whether it's appropriate or not. *And that's the rub*. Many Big Talkers are puzzled as they stand by and watch the deterioration of one relationship after another, as over the months and years they find it more and more difficult to communicate with the important people in their lives.

Once, when the three of us were together, Debbie remarked that she felt she had no one to talk with anymore. "I don't have many really close friends," she said, "and Bob turns off half the time we're together." Bob countered with, "What the hell, Debbie ... either you're ranting and raving about something *I've* done, or else you're ranting and raving about something someone else has done. Either way, you're not exactly what I'd call a 'fun' person to be with."

And there you have it. Although one of our current cultural injunctions is to "let it all hang out," to act honestly and spontaneously according to our feelings, and although letting it all hang out is probably on the whole a lot more healthy than holding it back, keeping it in, letting it *all* hang out *all* the time may have its consequences. Big Talkers like Debbie may or may not be comfortable with the way they express their anger. Either way, they need to be aware of how it can affect others so that they can decide when, where, how much, and even *if*, big talking is appropriate.

Debbie is one of those Big Talkers who continues to get angry enjoyment from an incident by replaying it over and over again to anyone who will listen; she reproduces a scene with all the emotion she can muster.

Others simply explode, after which the incident is forgotten. Mark, a sixteen-year-old I know, is like this. Mark flies off the handle quickly and is just as quick to forgive and forget. I've heard Mark give vent to five or ten minutes of heavy verbal anger and then grin and say, "Okay. Got that one off my chest."

Mark's family and close friends know that his outbursts are always followed by calm and reasonable understanding. Unfortunately, though, his teachers and some of the kids at school don't. He's having a tough time of it there and has been thrown out of the classroom on several occasions because of what the school principal calls Mark's "uncontrollable bad temper."

Mark's mother is worried. "He's a good boy, not unstable, not violent. But how can you get other people to understand?" The answer, unfortunately for Mark and his mother, is "You can't." Most other people, the ones who don't already know and love Mark, aren't going to want to invest the time and effort it would take to really understand him. Mark will have to recognize this. When he does, perhaps he will decide to modify his behavior and get out of his anger rut.

If you live with or are closely involved with an exploder like Mark, it might be helpful to know that these people *need* a receptacle for their anger. If the recipient moves away, turns a deaf ear, the exploder gets even angrier. (What you do with this information, of course, is up to you.) Also, exploders need to be respected for the validity and intensity of their emotions. (Sometimes, the Big Talker who does it in a monotone is separated from his feelings.)

Another kind of Big Talker is the Leaker. Leakers verbalize their anger, but only in little dribs and drabs, and often with a smile. Should anyone be perceptive enough to recognize the anger in what the Leaker says, and remark on it, the Leaker will probably react with hurt surprise.

Typical Leaker comments:

"Your new slacks suit is great . . . but isn't it just a little snug through the hips?"

"Marilyn's boy friend seems awfully nice, though personally I'd never want to get involved with a musician."

"I'm so happy to hear that Tom got into Yale. But I hear it's not all that difficult these days because so many people are sending their kids to the state universities."

The Leaker, whether he or she is aware of it or not, discharges anger by talking *about* others.

I'm thinking now of Babs, a woman in her middle thirties, who has a whole army of friends, more friends, in fact, than anyone can possibly be a friend *to*, and who always has some nice, kind word to say about each of them:

"Roberta is a true friend ... she really goes out of her way for you."

"Ann is such a super cook ..."

"Rosemary has a marvelous sense of humor ... what a comedian."

Then, suddenly, when you least expect it and just before her paean of praise has come to a conclusion, she injects the anger. Sometimes, but not always, it's preceded by a "but":

Roberta (the true friend) "has a neurotic need for people."

Ann (the cook) "has nothing better to do with her time."

Rosemary (the comedian) "isn't very attractive, so she *has* to be a clown."

The dig is there, the needle has been jabbed, Babs has unloaded some of her anger, and the funny thing is, she's not even aware of what she's done. Her jabs, though, are never terribly destructive, and her friends have learned to accept her little leaked-out angers, so it seems to work for everyone.

First cousin to the Leaker is the Truth-Teller. Like Leakers, Truth-Tellers unburden themselves of angry feelings in somewhat devious, round-about ways, and again like the Leaker, a Truth-Teller may be unaware of the anger motivating his or her words. All the same, what the Truth-Teller calls "honesty" is really anger in disguise.

Truth-Tellers feel free to say anything at all as long as it's the truth.

When you're feeling down, and you look it, the Truth-Teller will be the first to comment on your appearance: "Gee, Louise, you look just awful. Are you sick or something?"

When someone you know is planning a party, and *you* haven't been invited, the Truth-Teller feels you ought to know about it: "Gee, Louise, I really think it's rather strange that Ariadne didn't ask you to her cocktail party. I thought the two of you were the best of friends."

When your husband gives your friend a lift home from work, the Truth-Teller finds a way to pass the information on to you: "Gee, Louise, I saw Bill and Betty together in the car yesterday afternoon. It must be awfully nice when your husband is genuinely fond of your friends. *My* husband can't tolerate most of my friends."

Truth or anger? Most Truth-Tellers would deny that anger lurks behind their honesty, and there's probably not much point in trying to convince them otherwise. However, I think it's ironic that these people who are so anxious to make *you* aware of the truth, the whole truth, and nothing but the truth can be so dishonest to themselves about their own feelings.

Which brings us to the sub-species of Big Talker I like to call the Commentator. A lot of modern young parents—in fact, a lot of modern young people who read and unfortunately misinterpret books like this one—fall into this category.

Commentators are convinced that suppressing anger (or any other emotion) is bad for them, and they work very hard at learning to express themselves. But, however much in earnest these people may be, they're so far from knowing what they *really* feel that they're like robots, responding on cue in the way they think they ought to respond. The emotion itself is missing.

Perhaps the best example I can give of a Commentator in action involves a conscientious young mother who wants her four-year-old son to grow up whole and in touch with *his* feelings. She believes, and rightly so, that if the boy sees her being honest about *her* feelings, he will not fear being honest about *his*.

One day, she brought him to my house for a visit. I poured a glass of milk for the child. He drank most of it and then, either out of carelessness or maybe it was deliberate, he spilled the rest. The mother looked up from her coffee, blinked a couple of times, and in a deadpan monotone said, "Keith, I am angry at you for spilling your milk."

Keith and I both looked at her in bewilderment. Was she angry, or not? If she was, her words and tone of voice certainly didn't fit the feeling. If she wasn't, and I suspect this was the case, then why bother to say anything at all? Far from giving her child the benefit of seeing honest emotion, honestly expressed, this young mother succeeded only in confusing him.

The point, of course, is that you can't borrow either your words or your emotions from books and expect them to have any authenticity. To express your anger is a truly liberating experience. But first you have to learn to *feel* it.

Finally, there is the Verbal Self-Hater (VSH). The VSH is a close relative of the Corner Person. Both hate themselves. But whereas the Corner Person loathes quietly in the dead of night while tossing and turning in his bed, the VSH gets some measure of relief by talking about it, telling anyone who will listen how he has messed up his life, wife, career, friends, children, everything. In other words, private guilt isn't enough for the VSH. Only public self-excoriation will do.

The VSH can't stand himself, but he hopes that other people will like him, or at least tolerate him, if he establishes himself as the lowest, most incompetent and inconsequential person on the totem pole.

A VSH is happiest in a large group, because there he can unload the most anger at himself, in front of the most people. Being on TV in prime time on a major network, telling, through tears of anger, how very, very bad he is, would be the ultimate glory for such a person.

At a definite advantage over some of the other Self-Haters of the world, the VSH can get it all out, out, out into the open with his verbal hatchet jobs which means that this type rarely feels the need to self-destruct through alcohol, drugs, or suicide. The deed is done by words instead.

The problem, of course, is that after a while, people begin to take him at face value; he may actually talk his wife, kids, boss, and friends into believing he's almost as loathesome as he says he is and, one by one, they'll either walk off or find some other way to get him out of their lives. And while the VSH may need to hate himself, he doesn't need *that*.

Are You a Big Talker?

Did you find yourself here in this gallery of anger-types? Assuming you did, keep in mind that you talk for a reason. You talk because words help you get rid of your angry feelings. You have an outlet, and you use it, and that's good.

However, bear in mind that Big Talkers who

never do anything with their anger *but* talk it out in one particular way or other are going to put their feet in their collective mouths at least some of the time. That's fine, too, if you can handle the anger you get in return.

Even better, though, is to learn how to decide when (and how much) and with whom to talk and when to switch to some other mode of dealing with angry feelings.

1. One of the best ways is to LISTEN. Listen to them (the other people) and listen to the words forming in your mind. Try to hear what you're going to say before you say it. Don't make any attempts at editing, however. Just listen, then talk. As you talk, listen to your tone of voice. How do you feel about what you hear?

2. Just as important, listen to the other person's response. Really concentrate on what he or she is saying. Allow it to sink in before you make your reply.

After you've been listening for a while, you may discover (as many others have) that you've begun to automatically edit yourself, that where once you talked first and thought about what you said later, you're thinking first, selecting your words, deciding what to say and how to say it, holding back occasionally, letting go when circumstances warrant it. In short, you're getting out of your anger rut.

Big Talkers are okay if they have a "safe audience." Mark talked like crazy at home, but not at school. If married to, or involved with, a Big Talker, enjoy their release. But don't be drowned by it.

The Blamer

"I hate to sound holier-than-thou, but the truth of the matter is the only time I get angry is when someone provokes me."

A Blamer

"Sure, I get angry once in a while, but it's always *her* fault."

Another Blamer

What the two Blamers quoted above are doing is "projecting." I like the term because it so perfectly and graphically describes its own meaning. In projecting, the responsibility for the way one acts or feels is "thrown off" onto another person. People who project (and I'm not referring to home movies now) cannot or will not be held accountable for their own actions. They often sound as though they have no wills of their own. Whatever they do, it's because someone else *made* them do it. In fact. "He (or she) *made* me do it" is a favorite phrase of theirs. They're full of blame. Which is why I call them Blamers.

Phrases the Blamer likes to use are:

They're driving me crazy.

There must be something wrong with *him*.

She'll be sorry.

The Blamer's bag of anger is not necessarily any bigger or smaller than other people's. Its size and even its contents are less important than the way the Blamer dumps the whole thing into the lap of anyone who will take it. Most people don't want it and for obvious reasons (it's hard enough to cope with one's own bag of anger, let alone drag around the additional burden of someone else's) .

But occasionally, the Blamer does find someone who is not only willing to pick up that bag of anger, but accepts it with something like *joy*. This is the Self-Hater who is only too happy to find another person to share in his loathing for himself. Together, the Blamer and the Self-Hater make a sad but nevertheless near-perfect couple. Their needs and wants are neatly dovetailed, with the Self-Hater gladly occupying the role of scapegoat for the Blamer, while the Blamer flings ever more muck into the swamp of guilt and recrimination in which the Self-Hater loves to wallow. Strong language, perhaps, but one has only to watch this pair in action to know it is not very far off the mark.

Joe and Sheila are such a pair. A dark-haired, impeccably groomed good-looking man, about forty years old, Joe is plagued by the "if onlys." If only Sheila hadn't wanted to get married when they were both barely out of college, he could have knocked around Europe for a while and maybe studied art. If only she'd used proper birth control, they wouldn't have had three children right off the bat and he wouldn't have felt pressured to play it safe by staying on at his job with his father's company. If only Sheila hadn't gotten so sick that one year, they might have some money in the bank now. If only Sheila were more like his mother, the house wouldn't be such a mess all the time and it would be a pleasure to come home at night. And so on. And on.

As for Sheila, she accepts total responsibility for "messing up Joe's life." "If it wasn't for me, who knows what he might have become?" she mourns.

"But he loves me," she quickly adds. "He could have left me, but he stayed with me. I'm lucky to have him."

What neither of them understand is that Joe needs Sheila at least as much as Sheila needs Joe. Though he has several times threatened to "get out of this dead-end marriage," he ultimately always decided against it. "I can't explain it exactly," he says, "but even with all our problems, Sheila and I are tied together." Someplace deep inside he knows that without Sheila, he'd have to come to terms with life and assume responsibility for himself.

Joe's anger problem has nothing to do with being unaware of the emotion. He knows very well when he's angry, and like most other Blamers I've met, he's more than willing to talk about it, about the feeling and the way he handles it. He can do a fifteen-minute monologue, the point of which is that, yes, he's angry a lot, but his anger is always justified. He sees himself as an okay guy, just minding his own business and always trying to do what's right and good. It's *they* (and for Joe, "they" is Sheila, his parents, his children, and an assortment of neighbors, friends, and co-workers) who are wrong. In a sense, his blaming is healthy because it allows him to discharge anger energy (which puts him several notches on the anger scale above those unfortunates who turn their rage back upon themselves).

Even so, the Blamer is frequently a miserable person for the simple reason that hardly anyone, except the Self-Haters, can tolerate having him around for long.

Poor Blamer. He started off no different from most other children whose parents disapproved of anger. Like other kids in similar situations, he learned that to express his feelings honestly was out of the question because, well, you never could tell what Mom and Dad would do to you if you did. His special way of adapting was to wiggle out of any unpleasantness by claiming it was "the other person's fault." The child who insists he didn't get a good grade on a math test because the teacher doesn't like him may be telling the truth. But he may also be a budding Blamer.

It isn't easy to deal with a Blamer. Some Blamers are so adept, make such good cases for themselves, have such convincing arguments, and such a high moral tone that they can twist almost any set of facts or circumstances into the form that best suits their purposes. For some, skillful blaming is a technique for success.

Almost every office has its resident Blamer—the executive who never makes a mistake but is instead "misinformed" or misled by inaccurate information from some hapless underling, who either gets fired or is so mercilessly chewed out by the boss that he decides to leave. This kind of Blamer not only always manages to look good himself, but in passing his errors and his anger along to the next person in line, he protects his own position in the company hierarchy.

The Blamer holds on to anger just long enough to find an appropriate target, then hurls the blame.

Occasionally, the Blamer meets with a situation where there really is cause for blame. When this happens, he's out of luck. Blaming no longer works. His bluff is called. He finally has to confront the truth and *do* something himself.

I'm thinking now of a lawyer I know, a man in

his fifties. Married for twenty-five years, Frank has worked hard, had accumulated some money, and now that the children are off on their own, he wanted to get more fun out of life, to travel, take out a subscription to the opera, perfect his tennis and golf games. Frank wanted his wife Matty to join him in his activities. They'd grown apart over the years, he said, and now he wanted a closer relationship.

Matty, however, was content with her house, her garden, and her two Yorkshire terriers; in fact, she was so caught up with them that even the prospect of the opera, which she'd loved many years earlier, didn't stir her enough to want to budge from home.

The word "blame" kept cropping up in Frank's conversation as he described his present unhappiness at not having a companion to share in his interests.

"I blame her for refusing to go along with me. If she were a loving wife, she'd try to make me happy."

"I blame her for not going back to school or getting a job or doing something, anything, constructive with her time."

"I blame her for getting to be so stagnant . . . so . . . (he searched for a word and triumphantly found it) . . . dull!"

"I blame her for being emotionally dead at the age of fifty. I'm not going to follow her to the grave."

"I certainly see that you *do* blame her," I said. "And it's obvious you don't like what's happened. What do you suppose you're going to do about it?" His face showed momentary surprise. Apparently he hadn't seriously considered doing anything about it. "I don't know," he said.

Frank saw four alternatives for himself: live the rest of his life blaming Matty for his own unhappiness; force her to change; get a divorce; find someone else to share his interests. He decided he didn't want to waste any more time on blaming. Matty said she was happy with the way things were; she didn't want to change. Frank did not want to divorce Matty so he chose the fourth way out: he went about finding himself a woman friend with whom to share sex and other pleasures.

Matty may or may not have known about the other woman. Either way, she didn't seem to care and never asked Frank about his nights out. Frank stopped blaming her for being what she was, and his feelings toward her actually became more positive, more loving and tender. She was a good person after all, he decided, and she had as much right to stay at home as he had to indulge his interests.

The point of this is not that extramarital sex and companionship is the way to solve a problem—often it only creates new ones—but rather that only when the Blamer is realistic about his anger (or when, as in Frank's case, his blaming is valid) and is willing to assume responsibility can he begin to find ways to deal with his problems. If Frank had gone on blaming Matty instead of looking for ways out of his dilemma, the rest of his life would have been frittered away in frustration.

Blaming is a self-protective response. If you throw all the blame for your anger onto someone else, if you claim he (or she) *made* you say all those nasty things, then you don't have to feel you're a "bad" person and you can hope no one else sees you as "bad," either. If you blame all your own mistakes and misfortunes on people or circumstances over which you have no control, then you don't need to do anything about them yourself. Blaming others *seems* to guarantee the Blamer a blameless existence.

Blaming may at first appear to be "healthy" because, in the process of throwing responsibility for your anger onto someone else, you automatically get rid of some of your anger-energy. But if blaming does nothing to change the situation that made you angry in the first place (and usually it doesn't), you'll simply go right on blaming and may find yourself, like Frank, in a state of heightened and perpetual frustration which is very unhealthy indeed.

Remember that the chronic Blamer often is intensely disliked by others. I don't mean to imply that the goal is to be loved and respected by all. When your every word and deed is calculated to win someone else's approval, when you live your life according to what you *think* will please others, (1) you lose sight of what pleases you, and (2) your efforts may be wasted because you can never know for sure what really will please all those others. Blaming, however, is a particularly unappealing and obnoxious form of behavior and most of us have a normal, healthy tendency to avoid those people who indulge in it with any regularity. If you're aware of this and can accept it instead of merely being puzzled (or angered) by the way others keep their distance, then you may choose to go right on blaming.

But what if you're a Blamer and you want to change? The first thing to do is ask yourself: Am I blaming in order to avoid responsibility? If so, why am I avoiding responsibility? What would I lose by assuming responsibility? What would I gain? Or is my blaming truly "justified"—i.e., is someone else preventing me from doing/being/getting what I want? If so, is blaming the best I can do? Would some other way of handling my anger get better results?

Are You a Blamer?

1. Think back to the last time you played the Blamer (perhaps, like Frank, or like Joe whom we met at the beginning of this section, your anger and your blaming are linked to an ongoing situation). Write a story describing the events that led up to your anger. Don't identify the characters, however—make up names or use initials instead—and stick to the truth as you perceive it. Go into detail about how that other person made you angry and why you blame him/her for what happened. Be specific about what the other person said and did and about your own reactions. When you're finished, put your story aside and reread it again in a few days. Given the circumstances, did each choose an appropriate way of handling their individual anger? Can you imagine other, better ways? Do you feel comfortable about the way the story ends? If so, why? If not, how do you wish it had ended?

2. Test your creativity. Next time you feel yourself revving up for a blame session, try to get through it without using the word "blame" or the phrases "You made me," and "It's your fault." In other words, go ahead and blame, but do it with new combinations of words.

3. Go through this book and pick out two or three ways of expressing anger that appeal to you, then imagine how it would feel to use them. Let's assume you chose "doing" as one of your favorite modes; think of a situation in which you blamed and then imagine being a Doer instead. Play the same game with some of the other anger-types you chose.

The Body Person

"I can actually feel myself getting sick when things start to go wrong in my life."
                                    A Body Person

Celia, a twenty-nine-year-old divorcee with two children told me that she had been getting frequent and intensely painful headaches ever since her ex-husband, Tony, and she had separated. She said she'd seen a doctor and he could find nothing physically wrong with her. The prescribed medication gave her some relief from pain. Still, Celia wanted to know *why* she was suddenly subject to these wretched headaches every week when "I used to have headaches only once or twice a *year*."

I suggested she "chart" her headaches by writing down everything that happened during the twenty-four hours before each one occurred.

A couple of months later, she said, "It sounds crazy, and I don't get the connection, but it seems that my headaches have something to do with my mother. She's been an angel ever since Tony and I split. I have a regular babysitter, but several times a week, Mom picks the kids up at school and watches them until I get home from work . . . anyway, my headaches only seem to come after she's been with the children."

I asked Celia if she and her mother got along well.

"Yes, I think we do," Celia answered. "And like I said, she's been an angel. She goes out of her way to help me out with the kids."

"Well, what about the children?" I asked. "How do they feel about spending so much time with your mother?"

"Oh, they like her fine," was the reply. Then, several seconds of silence. "There's one thing, though. She smacks them when they're fresh or naughty. I've never laid a hand on either of them. I don't like the idea of hitting defenseless little children. I have my own way of dealing with them when they get out of hand."

"Why don't you tell your mother that you'd rather she didn't hit the children," I suggested.

"I did, once," Celia said, "but she told me she used to slap *me* when I was bad and that physical punishment was the only thing that made any impression on children."

"Maybe you're angry at your mother because of the way she deals with the children," I said. "Maybe that's why you're getting these headaches."

Celia quickly dismissed the idea. "Angry? At my mother? When she's been so helpful? I don't think so. I certainly don't *feel* angry."

But a few months later, when her mother had gone to spend the winter in Florida with a friend, Celia remarked that she wasn't getting as many headaches as before.

Celia is a Body Person. She hates her anger so much that she suppresses any consciousness of it and at the same time she punishes herself for it. She gives herself headaches.

In the Body Person, anger sneaks around searching for a niche, a corner, a weak spot. Many of us have a "weak spot." Some people catch cold frequently, others are prone to skin deseases, still others get colitis, an ulcer, or suffer from high blood pressure. An enormously wide range of illnesses often can be traced to emotions, especially anger not squarely and honestly faced.

Does this mean that these ailments aren't *real*, or that you don't need to see a doctor if you develop symptoms? Absolutely not. Your ailment is very real and you definitely should have a medical check-up whenever you're not feeling well. However, as you become more aware of the way anger can affect your body, and you are more in touch with your feelings, your health may improve.

From time to time I meet someone who in effect says, "But this idea that anger can give you a headache, a stomachache, asthma, arthritis . . . it doesn't make sense. I don't believe it. Not unless you can prove it." To this I can only say we can't prove it, not yet. But more and more, evidence supporting this theory is causing medical researchers to react against the rational twentieth-century tendency to split "mind" (i.e., emotion, feeling, thought) and "body" and to view the two as parts of an interrelated whole, each portion greatly affected by the other.

Feelings that aren't acknowledged openly will make themselves known somehow, some way. When you consider anger as energy, and then think of an enormous amount of it accumulating in a rather complex, sensitive but well-plugged container, the body, then you can understand how pressure from unreleased energy can be built up to such a degree that the container is ruptured and can even explode.

The concept of anger as energy is more than just a metaphor. Physiologists now know that the human body is equipped with a kind of automatic self-protective system which, when triggered by anger or fear or any really intense emotion, increases the individual's strength and endurance. This mechanism, sometimes called the "fight or flight" reaction, dates from the time when our ancestors had no recourse but to deal with all threats in one of two ways: they either stood their ground and fought, or else they ran like crazy.

In the twentieth century, we try to cope with most of our problems by "thinking them through," but our bodies are still equipped with this "fight or flight" mechanism, and it works now as it did millions of years ago: a threat is perceived and physiochemical changes immediately begin to take place; sugar pours into the blood-stream, adrenaline is secreted, blood pressure is increased, and the heart beats faster, etc. At this point, the body is in a supercharged state, ready for action, *needing* action to dispel abnormal muscular tension and use up the over-supply of various substances dumped into the bloodstream to tide it over the "emergency."

And then ... nothing. We hold back. The body wants to move, go, do. The mind says unh-unh, no, stay still. The two, mind and body, are at war. Usually, the mind wins. Which means that all those chemicals have no place to go, all those muscles, tensed for action, stay tensed.

Though there are a number of different explanations, there is still some debate as to precisely how and to what extent these short-circuited physiochemical reactions affect our health. But it is generally agreed that they do, and that many common illnesses can be traced to the mind-body war.

Let's consider the common cold, for example. Current medical theory has it that we carry cold viruses inside us all the time. Why, then, do we catch cold at some times and stay cold-free at others? We say we "come down with something" when our resistance is low and cite circumstances, such as being "cold and tired." But then why doesn't everyone who comes back from skiing or ice skating, teeth chattering and utterly exhausted, immediately catch cold?

Some researchers are convinced that emotion—state of mind—has something to do with the answer, and that the body's ability to do battle with viruses and such is much more significantly hampered by an ongoing war with the mind than it is by getting cold or being tired.

It seems to explain why an exuberant skier or ice skater can maintain an immunity to cold viruses, no matter how chilled or exhausted he or she may be, while the person who is upset, in turmoil, anxious and torn by conflict, or just normally "low" or "blue," can almost count on coming down with a cold (or something else) to compound his problems.

The very language of anger tends to have pointed references to the physical and indicates that deep down at some unconscious level we're aware of a tie-in between our emotions and our bodily well-being. We talk, for example, about being "blind with rage," "blowing our stacks," or not being able to "swallow our anger." We say we're "itching to get our hands on somebody," and sure enough, many itchy skin diseases are suspected to be psychosomatic in origin.

We say that someone with whom we're angry is a "pain"—in the neck, in the behind, or just a pain. I actually worked with a man who had an on-again, off-again pain in the neck: on, whenever he got tense and angry, off, at other times. In his particular behavior code, anger was bad, and it eventually became clear that he literally gave himself these pains in the neck as self-punishment for harboring those "bad" angry feelings.

Other Body People I've known repaid themselves for their anger by giving themselves weak stomachs (digestive disturbances), weak bowels (diarrhea), the suffocating misery of asthma (they're so stuffed with anger, there's hardly room enough left in their bodies to draw in a breath). One woman I know "gave" herself a car accident. (A fifty-year-old with three grown sons and a husband she insisted she "adored" despite his frequent, open infidelity to her, had recently met a man who was not only interesting, but interested in her. At the time of her accident, she was on her way to meet this man, and perhaps sleep with him. Halfway to their rendezvous, her car swerved, for "no good reason," she says, and hit a telephone pole. Later, she told me that she knew the moment it happened that she was "paying for considering something bad.")

I've known other Body People who run from doctor to doctor, searching for one who will "cure" their stiff neck, or their migraine headaches, or their asthma or arthritis, or whatever, and the sad part is, it's a hopeless quest. When unacknowl-

edged anger is at the bottom of an illness, no pills
or injections or other medical treatment will
"cure" it, though the patient may experience
temporary relief. Only in confronting that anger,
staring it in the face, *feeling* it, accepting it as not
bad and as a part of oneself, does the real cure
begin.

Are You a Body Person?

If you absolutely adore your spouse, mother, father, brothers, sisters, children, co-workers, and all
the neighbors up and down the block, if you consider yourself a good, kind, loving, giving person
and *always* try to act accordingly, if you've never,
ever allowed yourself to feel a strong surge of anger flow through your body, chances are your anger has disguised itself as a physical ailment.
What's your weak spot? Where does it hurt?

The Body Person is someone who wants desperately to maintain a good, sweet, kind, lovable self-
image. To admit that he or she is angry is the
same as admitting that they are none of the things
they so much want to be. But while they can fool
their own heads, and do a bang-up job of fooling
the world at large, they can't fool their bodies.

How can the Body Person change?

1. First, and this is the hardest part of all, understand that being angry, thinking angry thoughts,
having angry feelings, doesn't make you evil.

Imagine that you are free to dislike (be angry
at) someone, *anyone*. Who is the first person to
pop into your mind? (Try not to censor your
thoughts. It's *okay* to be angry at a husband or
wife, a child, an in-law, a parent. Being angry is
not the same as hurting, destroying, killing. Anger

is a *feeling*, not an act.) If no particular face pops into your mind, no particular name comes to your lips, it doesn't mean you are not angry at anyone; it means you haven't reached the point where you can allow yourself to feel angry. Try the imagining game again in two or three days or so.

2. When you're able to focus your anger on some person (and don't worry about whether your anger is "justified" or not), carry on imaginary conversations with him or her. Include phrases such as:

I am angry at you because _____ (fill in the blank, no matter how petty or silly or unjustified your reason seems to you).

I want to do what *I* want to do, which is _____.

I don't want to do that because _____.

I can't be good and kind and considerate *all* the time. I have a right to _____.

I'm human. I have feelings, too, and my feelings tell me _____.

3. Next, here's a good exercise, one I've recommended to many patients: turn up the TV until it's blasting full volume. Then, *scream*. Put every ounce of your strength into these screams. Really exercise your lungs. (If you're worried about the neighbors, do your screaming into a pillow.) Scream until you're hoarse and can't scream anymore.

Naturally, this is just a way to get started. If your anger has been bottled up so long that you've developed physical symptoms such as migraines, asthma, rashes, diarrhea, constipation, etc., these simple exercises aren't going to change your body, your feelings, or your life overnight. But with them, you can begin to accept that the other side of loving is to occasionally feel angry as well.

The Comedian

Comedian: "What's a six-course Irish meal?"
Straight Man: "I don't know . . . what is a six-course Irish meal?"
Comedian: "A six-pack of beer."

A good deal of humor carries an enormous amount of anger with it. So much so that I begin to squirm and feel defensive even as I type out the ethnic joke above.

Obviously, if it's an Irishman telling the joke to another Irishman, it's okay, a light self-putdown. There's anger there, all right, but it's mixed with irony and turned back against the teller, his family, his fellow countrymen, his *group*. We're good sports, it says. We may not be perfect; we have our faults, but we're tough enough and strong enough to laugh at ourselves.

But if anyone else tells the joke, it becomes an ethnic slur. The humor isn't lost, but the hostility is heightened and directed outward—in this case at a whole group of people rather than back at the teller. It makes a distinction between "us" and "them."

Putting someone else down is a way of elevating oneself. Putdown humor often is a way of being "in," of solidifying your own position within a group and at the same time putting some vertical distance between yourself and your group, between "them" and "their group."

Hearing a Comedian put someone else down is, for some people, almost as good as originating the putdown oneself. Which is one reason for the popularity of the so obviously angry humor of comedians such as Don Rickles, whose commonest joke-form is the one that results in the humiliation of a rival. The pleasure comes from hearing someone being knocked. Of course, the Don Rickles brand of humor is not everyone's cup of tea and is, in fact, considered offensive by many who prefer instead the *self*-knocking Woody Allen mode. It wouldn't be fair of me to characterize Mr. Allen as a Self-Hater (I've never met the man), but there does seem to be an element of self-hate in some of the other Comedians who, like Mr. Allen, consistently make themselves the butt of their own jokes. Instead of going off into private self-hating binges, like other Self-Haters, these people indulge their loathing for themselves in public. Here again, the audience gets its kicks in hearing someone knocked and in this case, the comedian.

However, interesting though the professional comedian may be, I'm less concerned here with the person who makes a living out of being funny (not a bad way to use your anger), than I am with those people whose primary *personal* means of expressing anger is through humor. Almost everyone knows at least one private-life comedian, someone whose conversation is liberally salted with wisecracks, puns, clever retorts, and original jokes, and who doesn't use words to communicate so much as he uses them to spar. These people are often "popular" in the sense that they're good at parties. Their animated talk keeps things lively and "fun." But when one listens very carefully it is often possible to detect an angry, bitter tone underlying the witty top note.

Joy, a young woman I know, married a Comedian (for some as yet unidentified reason, male Comedians appear to outnumber female). Joy told me she married Barry because she fell in love with his sense of humor. "I'm not an especially funny person, myself," she said, "but I love to laugh and I've always been attracted to people who can tell jokes and make quick, witty remarks. Barry was always the center of attention at parties and I used to feel very proud and happy to be his date.

"What I didn't realize until quite a while after we were married was that Barry is an incredibly hostile person. I'd always imagined that any person who's so good at making other people laugh would be easygoing and good-natured. But I guess it isn't so. Not with Barry. He's funny but it's always at someone else's expense. These days, usually *mine*. His new party routine is something he calls the 'Joy and Barry' show. He does it like a TV situation comedy, and he goes on and on about our personal problems, including our sexual difficulties. He plays both parts, himself and me, but he always makes me out to be an ass. I tried to be a good sport about it and laugh along with everyone else, but I just don't enjoy being raked over the coals in public and I'm beginning to hate him for it.

"Recently I told him, with a smile and as nicely as I could, that I wished he'd stop making jokes about our marriage and especially about what we do in bed. He turned around and told me I was always a 'stiff' and I had a lousy sense of humor. It was the beginning of a horrible, vicious fight."

Barry operates in a way that's typical of many angry Comedians. Full of venom, he stings the object of his anger with humor. His purpose is not so much to amuse as it is to make the victim writhe in pain. In protesting, as Joy did, the victim plays right into the Comedian's hands; he then feels free to further denigrate the victim for being overly sensitive, for not being able to take a joke.

The natural-born Comedian, whose wit is effortless and whose mind and tongue work as one, producing a steady stream of satiric anecdotes, wisecracks, and original jokes, is a formidable opponent indeed, able to goad with gentle irony on the one hand or launch a slashing verbal attack that leaves his victim utterly defeated and gasping in disbelief. (A really witty man in business knows full well the power of his ridicule against someone with whom he is in battle for control. I've known several such men, and I've seen them go farther faster with their wit than they ever could have through more conventional power plays.) What makes humiliation through humor so annihilating is that most of us do not often have command of the quick retort required to get us off the hook. Who among us could, for example, muster the instant comeback of Benjamin Disraeli who, after Gladstone said to him, "Sir, you will die either upon the gallows or of venereal disease," immediately replied, "I suppose that depends on whether I embrace your principles or your mistress." (A commentator later said of this verbal duel that it was "about as playful as a cobra that's been poked with a stick.") In other words, the Comedian has the knack of putting others on the defensive; yet, unless one is a Disraeli, or a Comedian oneself, there is no defense.

The Comedian "gets away with it" because everyone supposedly understands that his attacks are, after all, "all in fun." The victim loses doubly if he/she isn't "big enough to take it." So most victims do try to be "big enough to take it." At a recent social gathering, a middle-aged woman I'll call Ginny was spewing out a stream of humorous anecdotes involving her close friend Leslie. More specifically, Ginny was recounting Leslie's very real trepidations about going out on her first job interview in years, her indecision over what to put in her résumé, whether or not to fudge her age and her previous work experience, her ruminations over skirt lengths, how to wear her hair, and how much makeup to put on. Leslie has a soft, drawling voice and a very slight stutter, and Ginny, who probably should have been on the stage, played her to perfection, at the same time making her look not only indecisive but somewhat cowardly and vain as well. This all took place in front of a gathering of five or six people, and poor Leslie, a feeble grin on her face, stood right next to Ginny the whole time. Later, I met Leslie coming out of the bathroom. Her eyes were reddened but she smiled.

Probably nowhere is the anger/humor connection so evident as in the practical joke, though here again the victim who isn't "big enough to take it"—the humiliation and the discomfort of being made the butt of a joke—comes off as a spoilsport. The "humor" is a practical joke—from the most sophisticated and elaborate setup right on down to the kind that depends on cheap novelty-store gimmicks (drinking glasses that leak, wind-up false teeth, etc.)—arises almost entirely out of viewing the victim's shocked disbelief. The greater the initial shock and discomfort, the "funnier" the joke. Which is probably why the classic pie-in-the-face continues to be such a favorite. In fact, as of now there are at least two pie-throwing outfits which, for a fee of about $35, will smash a banana cream delight into the face of your husband, wife, boss, best friend, next-door neighbor, or whoever else you feel deserving of the honor. Don Murdock, the head of Pie Face International (one of the companies), says that his business is booming because the present economic slump has put people in a "retaliatory" mood. As for the possibility of someone who's been hit in the face with a banana cream pie retaliating, Murdock says he isn't worried about legal repercussions. "A civil suit would make the guy who files it look like a bloody fool and give us a million dollars worth of publicity." In the same article, Comic Soupy Sales explains that pie throwing is funny because "for a couple of moments it turns the big guys into slobs, puts them on the same level as everyone else."

Angry humor can be as flat-footed and simple-minded as a pie in the face, or as subtle and razor-sharp as a Disraeli riposte. In either case, and in all the gradations in between, it is generated by tension, hostility, resentment, which are converted in the Comedian's body and mind into the sly jest, the cagey putdown, the cleverly turned anecdote, or the practical joke that relieves tension for the Comedian and for his audience as well. So, while the Comedian may indeed inflict occasional misery and embarrassment on others, he has a way of dealing with his emotions that is valid and useful to him. If his antics don't cross over into the realm of outright and direct aggression, he is rewarded by appreciative laughs. The Comedian is often and understandably reluctant to give up his personal mode of handling anger, and again, assuming his wit stops short of inflicting real misery, there is very little reason why he should.

Freud says laughter in general is the free discharge of psychic energy heretofore employed in areas in which discharge has been inhibited. No question that jokes and laughter, along with weeping and swearing, do have a purgative, "laxative" effect on the emotions, both for the joker and sometimes for the jokee, too.

Aggressive laughter can be a delicious way of living with annoyance, frustrations, disappointments, failures; it discharges the repressed psychic energy of resentment. And if we can learn to laugh at ourselves, not put ourselves down, not become Self-Haters, but manage to deflect the anger and pain we feel at viewing life's inequities and convert them instead into belly laughs and guffaws, so much the better. "A vain, frightened, angry man," says one philosopher, "can never laugh at himself." Which is not to say that those who see no humor in the human condition are by definition vain, frightened, and angry, but that we might feel less anger, fear, and crippling self-consciousness if we could make the attempt to take ourselves less seriously.

Are You a Comedian?

If you have the ability to make others laugh, if you have a reputation for being quick, witty, clever, you probably also employ humor as a way of expressing and dealing with your anger.

It's a viable mode, one of the best, in fact, but it can be overused and abused.

You may discover, after giving the matter some thought, that you are always taking aim at one particular person and making him or her the butt of your jokes over and over again. If so, you probably ought to reexamine your relationship with this person. What makes you feel the need to punish him or her? What is it that he or she does (or represents) that brings on your anger? Is there anything you can do, or that the two of you can do together, to eliminate some of the bad feelings you engender in one another?

Are you so caught up in your role as Comedian, are you so compulsive about it that every single statement you make is twisted into a barbed "funny?" Then you should be aware that many people find the chronic joker exhausting to be with. There is a time for fun and games and a time when people expect and deserve straight, honest answers. In not recognizing and honoring the difference, you may be endangering the important one-to-one relationships in your life. You might also consider the possibility that in always being the wisecracking Comedian, you are actually avoiding direct communication which always has an element of confrontation with others in it.

Finally, although being a Comedian gets you lots of attention (which is one reason you cling to the role—almost everyone loves the limelight), you should also recognize that stinging, hurtful remarks tend to be a turnoff, not only for the person at whom they are directed, but for the rest of your audience as well. Though you may take great pride in what you like to feel is your cleverness and wit, there is always the possibility that other people see you mainly as "cruel" or "vicious," a verbal bully.

Don't stop the funny business; we need all the laughter we can get. But do try to expand your range of expression. The following anger exercises will get you started:

1. Be conscious of the quality of your humor. How much of it is really hurtful? (One way to gauge the degree of malice is to ask yourself: "How would I feel if that remark were directed toward *me*?") You might even keep a mental count for a week or so, rating your various funnies as (a) genuinely amusing and entertaining, (b) a means of revenge; getting even with someone, (c) downright mean and for no particular reason, and (d) an effort to relieve the tension of a difficult situation.

2. Zero in on your comic anger by watching the facial expression of the person to whom it is directed. Then watch to see what happens next. Does the conversation come to an abrupt halt? Does the other person immediately take the defensive? Are those laughs genuine? Or are they simply nervous titters, a way of covering up and getting through an embarrassing moment? Or what? Whatever the response, do you feel good about it? If so, why? If not, why?

3. Think back to the last time you were angry and you knew it and you expressed it with hostile humor. If you could relive the situation, what different mode of expression would you choose? Imagine yourself actually engaging in that other mode. How would it feel? How do you think the other person would react? Would the outcome have been better, or worse, than the real-life outcome of the incident?

The Corner Person

"I remember hearing my parents telling their friends what a 'good' child I was. Now I know what a terrible price I paid to get that praise."

A Corner Person

"I try not to get angry, not to express any anger. I have the feeling that if I do, I'll be punished."

Another Corner Person

"When I think back, I realize I was depressed as a child. I'm still depressed some of the time, but I'm working with it now."

A Third Corner Person

Corner People learn at a tender age that when you get angry and you do something that expresses your anger, you get sent to bed or to another room, or you have to stand in a corner, the better to contemplate and repent your bad behavior. (I met one middle-aged man who told me that his father actually made him a dunce cap; it was clapped on his head whenever his parents deemed him guilty of committing some gross and horrible infraction of the household rules, such as leaving the back door open, forgetting to hang up his coat and hat, being late to the dinner table, that sort of thing.)

The parents of Corner People often subscribe to the theory that if the sinner is left to sit it out alone, in silence, he will dwell on his wickedness, see the error of his ways, and ultimately reform himself. A neat theory, but one that doesn't translate so neatly into practice. In recent years we've begun to see that simply jailing the criminal to change his attitudes and behavior often begets *more*, instead of less, antisocial behavior. In the same way, and for many of the same reasons, we now know that calling a small child "bad," and encouraging him to view himself as "bad," doesn't promote the growth of a "better" individual. What one is apt to get instead is a human being convinced of his own "badness," and either hating the world for calling him "bad" and spending the rest of his life getting even (the criminal and other antisocial types) or hating himself and hiding his badness (the Corner Person).

Today's Corner Person, then, was yesterday's "jailed" child—the degree of his present secretiveness, depression, and self-hate corresponding more or less to the degree and method of the physical and/or emotional punishment to which he was subjected in the past.

If the Corner Person was indoctrinated with the belief that he was being bad when he talked back, tried to get his own way, or otherwise asserted himself, whenever he feels a small bubble of rage rising inside as an adult, he will beat his own hasty retreat, make for some safe haven like the bedroom, the den, the office on Sunday. There in his hiding place he is out of danger, protected from the possibility of an angry confrontation and the excruciating guilt he would experience if he vented his feelings. There in his hiding place he can sit and contemplate his badness, punish, blame, flagellate himself for stepping out of line, emotionally if not in word or deed.

"My parents were very religious and I was

brought up on the concept of turning the other cheek, to be passive and accepting when someone hurt my feelings or treated me badly." This, from a young woman I know called Jean, now thirty, who is only just beginning to question what she had learned about anger as a little girl.

"I went around feeling guilty all the time," she told me. "I was constantly apologizing to my parents, always saying 'I'm sorry' about something, sorry I was so clumsy and dropped a dish, sorry I was so stupid and couldn't pull straight 'A's,' sorry that I had the effrontery to ask for a bicycle . . ."

Jean is now aware that for many years her anger fed on itself. Having to say all those unnecessary "sorries" made her an angry child. But, in her home, anger was considered evil, which made *her* feel like an evil person, which led to more guilt and apologies, which made her even angrier. And so it went, on and on. Jean, of course, is a Corner Person, but the fact that she now recognizes that in hating her anger she hates herself indicates to me the possibility that she may someday be able to work her way out of the corner.

Another Corner Person, a young executive I'll call Eddie, is also in the process of learning to accept his anger. However, he still finds it difficult to deal with "differences of opinion."

He tells me that every so often, during a meeting or in some other business situation, he will come up with an idea or suggestion that is "better and more valuable than something someone else has contributed. But," he says, "it always seems to me that if I bring it up, there'll be an argument. So, I figuratively go to my room by shutting up. When this happens, I can actually see myself in my mind's eye, a little kid being sent to his room.

Now I feel even angrier about the way I was treated as a kid. Some of my energy, aggression, whatever you want to call it, which I need in this business I'm in, is stifled because of those early fears.

"Okay, I'm working on it, but I still don't feel easy and free about coming right out and disagreeing with someone. I can't say, 'No, I don't think your way. I think *my* way.' "

Another Corner Person who is trying to work her way out told me that as a child she was made to sit in a chair when she was "naughty." She sulked, but she never cried. "I simply wasn't going to give *them* [her parents] the satisfaction of seeing me in tears." She added, "To this day it's hard for me to cry about anything.

"With a guy, when something doesn't go my way, I sit in a chair and sulk, just like when I was a kid."

Still another Corner Person, a research biologist, explained that as a child she controlled and inhibited any expressions of anger in order to appease her parents, "to keep everything smooth and on an even keel.

"I don't remember ever having been sent to my room," she said, "but inside of me I think I'm what you call a Corner Person because I always locked my angry feelings up in a tight box. I still do. Maybe that's one reason why I chose lab work. I'm alone on the job most of the time and I don't have too much to do with other people. It's just me and the microbes and I don't have to deal with *them* on an emotional level."

There are a couple of variations on the basic Corner Person. First, the Drowner. Drowners are more likely than any other anger type to dull the anguishing hate they feel for themselves and their anger with alcohol or drugs.

A teen-ager, undergoing the pain of leaving home to become a person on his own, told me that he spent two whole years of his young life "stoned on grass, acid, uppers and downers, whatever I could get my hands on." He did it so he wouldn't have to think about his parents. He, too, had learned that it was bad to be angry and worse to express it, and, as he put it, "I hated my folks for laying all that shit on me."

But, even as he sat there stoned, his anger continued to bubble to the surface and he realized he had to choose between one of two alternatives: either confront the emotion or spend the rest of his life using drugs in the attempt to tune it out. He chose the first course.

But, one wonders, what about the literally millions of problem drinkers and other addicts who, unable to confront their anger and the feelings of worthlessness and self-hate that go along with it, continue in their efforts to drown their pain in alcohol or drugs?

For them, the guilt attached to the anger they feel, either free-floating anger, or, unthinkably worse (to them), anger focused on Mom or Dad, is so unbearable that the only way to get by at all is through a haze of numbness. These are Corner People who have carved a very special niche indeed for themselves.

Another kind of Corner Person is the Self-Destroyer who so despises the energy of his anger (again, because of what he learned about it as a child) that he takes that enormous bag of emotion, puts it all on top of his own head, and allows it to bury him, sometimes literally.

The Self-Destroyer is a victim of depression syndrome. His feelings of worthlessness and powerlessness have taken over, crowding out most if not all of his "good" self.

Naturally, different Self-Destroyers manage to damage themselves to different degrees and in different ways. In some people, self-loathing may manifest itself in the way they consistently invest unwisely and lose money on every venture. Others have a knack for ruining every personal relationship. Still others insulate themselves from the world and their pain with sleep, spending half the day and most of the night in bed, and still they suffer from "fatigue." (This horizontal method of blocking out anger is often abetted by a variety of sleeping pills.)

Eventually, some Self-Destroyers arrive at a point where they see no possible exit, no feasible way out of the torture of living, none but one. It is then that they decide to end it all with a bullet or perhaps by driving a car off the road, or with an overdose of sleeping pills.

I often think that if I could somehow magically round up all these suicidal Self-Destroyers and put each one in a room with full permission to scream out their hate, not only with their lungs but with their whole bodies, from toes on up to the tops of their heads, they would shake off some of the weight of their guilt and anger.

But, of course, once couldn't be enough. It would take years of shrieking and flailing around in those rooms to undo the hurt that was done so quickly and thoroughly, and perhaps with all good intentions, by those misguided giants who ruled over their earliest lives.

One woman, Lee, described to me the long,

silent days in her childhood home. There were six children, plus Mother. And then there was Father. (She spoke the word "Father" in a hushed, almost reverent tone, drawing it out and capitalizing it with respect.)

Father radiated disapproval. Everyone in the family, Lee said, felt the vibrations of displeasure and disappointment that emanated from him. None of them were good enough for Father. When one child's behavior fell short of the mark Father had set, or did something that Father considered disrespectful, or even forgot a small chore (like clearing the table), they all suffered.

Lee's sadness, as she related her story, was heart-rending. Her voice was a monotone, and she huddled in her chair as though cowering from the remembered frown on her father's face. At one point, I encouraged her to stand up and to speak with all the emotion she could muster. "What you feel, whether it's fear, rage, sadness, or something else, try to put some of that feeling into what you're saying," I urged.

She stood up and continued: "I remember that sometimes he would call us in, all of us together. He would sit in his chair, an enormous leather armchair, and he would point his finger at each of us in turn and tell us what we'd done to disappoint him. After he had recounted our misdeeds, he'd sentence us. 'I want you all to go up to your rooms and think over how bad you've been.' I would lie in my bed at night and think about my badness, and it seemed to me that I was the most wretchedly wicked child in the world . . ."

One of Lee's brothers is an alcoholic, another committed suicide. The other four, she told me, are in therapy, struggling to become "humans."

Lee is feeling much better about herself these days. From time to time she actually laughs while recounting stories from her childhood, and some of the anger and hate she felt for herself have been refocused on her father (or, rather, on his memory; he died four years ago). In the future, she may even learn to love herself and accept her anger, and when this happens, she will also undoubtedly be able to forgive her father who first set her on the road to self-hate.

Are You a Corner Person?

While most other anger-types, the Actors and the Comedians, the Doers and the Big Talkers, get some measure of relief in dealing with their emotions in the way that they do, the Corner Person gets only a bag of anger that becomes more monstrously difficult to bear as time goes by. There is absolutely nothing to be gained, and everything to lose, by converting one's anger-energy into self-hate.

If you're a Corner Person, if you almost never consciously feel angry at anyone but yourself, if you are frequently overcome by feelings of powerlessness, worthlessness, and self-loathing, the best anger exercise I can recommend is that you seek professional help.

If you have a drinking problem, are addicted to drugs, or engage in any other seriously self-destructive behavior or if you often entertain thoughts of suicide, I beg you, no, I *command* you, to see a therapist.

You may, on the other hand, be what I call a "borderline Corner Person." How do you know for sure? Obviously, it's impossible for me to make any accurate behavioral diagnosis via the pages of this book. But I can give you a rather sketchy portrait of this type. If it sounds very much like you, then you may belong to this group.

The very thought of an angry confrontation makes the borderline Corner Person (for brevity's sake, I'll use the initials BCP) feel uncomfortable, and he or she rarely if ever makes an outright declaration of anger, even to a third and supposedly neutral party. For example, the BCP probably wouldn't say, "I've had it with Sonia. She's always late." Instead, this type may take Sonia's lateness as a matter of course. This is because the BCP generally has a rather low opinion of himself or herself and assumes that Sonia shares it, in which case, why should Sonia bother about being on time?

With the BCP, anger is suppressed and/or turned back upon the self. Even righteous anger, the emotion that wells up within us when we either witness or are the victim of an obvious and clear-cut wrong, may be an alien feeling.

Since suppressed, unacknowledged anger is one cause of depression, the BCP experiences more than occasional blue periods. During these times he feels helpless and at the mercy of circumstances. He may also feel like a "lousy, no-good bum" (as one BCP I know described himself). However, the depressions come and go and are not accompanied by suicidal thoughts.

If you recognize yourself here, remember that therapy can help you feel better about yourself. But regardless of whether or not you decide to seek professional help, you may benefit from the following simple anger-exercises.

1. The very next time you are depressed, get a pencil and some paper and sit down in a quiet, private place. Try to let your mind go blank so that any thoughts or feelings that are lurking just below the surface will have a better chance to come up for an airing.

Now, very quickly, write "I am angry at _____ _____ (Fill in the blank). Who or what pops into your head? Once you've come up with a name or a set of circumstances, go into detail about the reason for your anger.

If your conscious mind denies being angry at the person whose name first occurred to you, write the name down anyway, and then try to decide how you really feel about that person. Do you wish that he or she were with you now? If so, why? If not, why not? When was the last time you saw that person? What happened then? Was it pleasant? Why? Was it unpleasant? Why?

Some Corner People can never seem to go beyond writing "I am angry at me (or myself) ." If this happens, ask yourself *why* you are angry at yourself and write down the reasons. Be specific. Don't write "I am angry at me because I am a no-good lousy bum." Write "I am angry at me because I forgot Tom's birthday." And then ask yourself why you are angry at Tom. Or, write "I am angry at me because I lost my job." And then ask yourself what it is about the job and the people with whom you work that makes you angry. Or write "I am angry at me because I'm a terrible son (or daughter) ." And then ask yourself why you're angry at your parents.

What I'm trying to get across here, of course, is that when you think you're angry at yourself, you may actually be reacting to a real person or set of circumstances. Once you begin to grasp this concept, you can stop being so hard on yourself.

2. This one may be difficult but I hope you can bring yourself to do it anyway. Complete each of the following:

I am angry at my mother because ＿＿＿＿＿＿.
I am angry at my father because ＿＿＿＿＿＿.

Don't censor yourself. Write whatever comes into your mind, no matter how far-out, seemingly far-fetched, unfair, or "ungrateful" it may seem. Neither your mother nor your father will ever see what you've written (unless you show them), so you needn't worry about "hurting" them, nor about making them angry in return.

If you pull a blank on either or both of these, try again in a few days. And keep trying until you can complete this exercise.

It's important for you to remember that *everyone* feels some anger at their parents and that you're no exception. Nobody is perfect, and parents, being human, are not perfect either. It's pointless to defend them by pretending that they are. More important, it's harmful to *you*. Because if *they're* perfect, then that means you can never attain their perfection, and that can make you feel even worse.

When you can see your parents as two people who, though perhaps kind and well-meaning, made some mistakes in raising you, when you can learn to be angry at them and maybe hate them a little and then go on from there to accept them and love them for what they are, with all their imperfections—only then will you be in a position to accept and love yourself.

The Creator

"I like to get a good argument going every once in a while ... it sort of relieves the monotony."

A Creator

"It's not that I'm always spoiling for a fight ... but I don't back off from one either ..."
Another Creator

"I have to admit it ... I get high on anger."
A Third Creator

Sometimes the hours of one's day flow on in orderly smoothness and it seems for a while that really all is right with the world. For most of us, the periods of relative tranquility are a much welcome respite to be savored, delighted in, while they last. Others can't take the calm, or at least not for very long. They're the Creators, the people who simply can't let well enough alone but instead have a real need to stir things up, make some choppy wavelets of anger.

It's almost as though the Creator doesn't know how to be in tune with himself and at peace with the world, and, in fact, the Creator is lacking in the ability to enjoy. Or, rather, what the Creator seems to enjoy is what most other people would rather do without: discordant, never-jangling, angry episodes.

One woman I know, married to a Creator, told me about the many times her husband would come home from his office "obviously looking for something to get mad about." "He paces around for a while," she says, "opening and closing the refrigerator, poking into closets, asking questions about what the kids have been up to, and how did my day go, until finally he lights on something he can get angry about. The other day he didn't find beer in the refrigerator and all hell broke loose. 'I bust my ass all day at the office and when I come home I want to relax,' he says, 'and then there's no beer and what kind of a house are you running here, Paula?' and so on and on. The truth is, most of the time there isn't any beer in the refrigerator and it doesn't bother him one bit. He just wants an excuse to let off steam."

I think Paula's last phrase is exactly right. The Creator's anger is such that he has to set about building, "creating" situations that allow him to get rid of some of it.

On the days when the sun shines, the meetings all get started on time, the traffic is not bumper to bumper, the kids are polite and cooperative, and the roast beef is cooked just right, the Creator begins to feel distinctly uncomfortable. He's a person with an especially large bag of generalized or "free floating" anger. The tension of that anger is always with him and it builds to unbearable proportions if he doesn't regularly unload it. So if in the course of a normal day he can't find some "valid" excuse for venting his feelings, he has to manufacture one. When you know this about a Creator, you begin to understand why he seems to take the bad times when nothing goes right, and he can actually pick and choose legitimate targets for his anger, in stride, while the good times trip him up.

How did he get that way? Well, for many Creators, it all started as usual way back when, in

early childhood. The Creator might have felt
abandoned; maybe he actually *was* abandoned
emotionally, in that Mom and Dad turned their
attention away from him and lavished it instead
on a younger (or brighter or cuter) brother or sister. Or maybe somebody died. Or his parents got
divorced. Or there were big financial problems.
Or the family moved around an awful lot. In any
event, life was full of anxiety for the poor young
Creator, and that anxiety never did go away but
got twisted into anger instead. Anger is somehow
easier to live with than chilling, ever-present
dread, but the tension it produces still must be
dissipated from time to time; hence, the Creator's
sometimes frantic search for an escape valve—he
needs it.

Other people develop this need to create later
on in life. One sees it often in people whose daily
routine doesn't provide enough positive personal
rewards. Housewives, for example. Consciously or
not, many young women begin to resent the unre-
mitting round of cleaning and cooking and chauf-
feuring and shopping for the family, the giving
and doing-for-others of their lives. Neither their
time nor their energy is their own, or so it seems,
and a baby's smile or a husband's appreciative
peck on the cheek don't seem fair and adequate
compensation for the endless giving. The young
housewife/mother who falls for the happily-ever-
after myth soon senses that she's been had, and it
makes her angry, and she needs to create quasi-
legitimate outlets for her anger (since she probably
can't allow herself to stand up and point her finger at her husband and children and yell, "I'm angry at you because I'm young and I've got energy
and ability and I want to have fun and do what *I*

want to do for a change but I've got the feeling that I'm supposed to wait on you hand and foot instead"). So, when the unsuspecting three-year-old is playing nicely off by himself, she swoops down on him for messing up her nice clean kitchen floor. Or when her husband is relaxing in front of the TV set, she berates him for never spending time with the children.

We can always find something the matter. Even when nothing specific is wrong, we can discover no end of things that are not exactly right. Therefore, the Creator doesn't often have to look far in order to find something upon which to hitch his anger. Frequently, he hitches it to a person. Almost anyone will do, but many Creators have a favorite scapegoat. When a child becomes the scapegoat, as is often the case, he or she may bear the scars for a lifetime.

A father of five children consistently picked on his eldest daughter. What motivated his choice? One can't know absolutely, but of all the kids in the family, her character (or parts of it) bore the most striking resemblance to his. (She was a quiet, careful, unadventurous child, just as he himself had been; he loathed her reticence and caution as he loathed them in himself.)

At any rate, the father focused much of his anger (and there was a lot of it) on this particular daughter. As the oldest girl, she bore much of the responsibility for the housework and this provided the setup for his anger. Each evening after work and all during the weekends, he hounded her: "Diane, did you iron my blue shirt?" "Diane, run out to the store and get me some cigarettes." "Diane, go help the younger children to clean up their rooms." Most of the time, Diane was docile and compliant, but when she did hesitate, even for an instant, he would pounce, calling her "lazy, stupid, ungrateful, selfish and bad."

The other children disliked their father (maybe "hated" would be a better word here), but not having themselves been the butt of his anger, they were not afraid of him and they grew up into relatively healthy, self-assertive adulthood. The wife was never the recipient of his anger, either; she had learned early in the marriage always to keep a certain aloof distance between herself and her husband. So it was only Diane who suffered. Singled out for reasons she had no way of comprehending, her self-esteem was so battered and crushed she eventually went into emotional hiding and became a kind of recluse, unable to risk adult relationships, frequently unable even to talk to people.

As with most Creators, the father's conscious intent never was to murder someone else's sense of being a valuable, worthwhile person, but this was the unfortunate result of the way he handled his anger. Motivated by a need to rid himself of his own excessive store of angry tension, he was blinded to its effects on others. This often happens with Creators, which is one reason that living with a Creator can be a difficult, sometimes dangerous proposition, especially for children, but also for those adults with an undeveloped sense of self-esteem. (Spreading one's anger around is at least better than dumping it on one person.)

Typically, the victim is accustomed to receiving anger which he or she didn't provoke, and begins to anticipate it and prepare a response in advance. In this respect the Creator may function like the man in the story who decides to borrow a neighbor's lawn mower. As he walks across the grass to the neighbor's house, it occurs to him that maybe his request will be refused. This makes him angry. With every step he takes, he gets angrier, and he's so furious by the time the neighbor answers the door that he bellows, "Keep your f——g lawn mower for all I care," and punches the poor bewildered fellow.

Take Maddy, for example. She recognizes that many times anticipation of someone else's negative response is what "primes" her for anger. She told me about the time she and her husband were considering various plans for the coming summer: "There were three or four places I really wanted to go," she said, "and though I wasn't at all sure that Tom would veto any of them, I got myself into a real state imagining that he *might*. By the time we actually sat down to talk, I was sure he'd reject all my ideas, and I was mad as hell. I said I wanted to go to Portugal in this nasty, hostile tone of voice, and, of course, he reacted badly, and we got into a fight, just as I knew we would. I guess I wanted that fight. I needed it. And I got it.

"Another time," she went on, "I got into a fight with the manager of a shoe store. I'd bought a pair of shoes, but when I tried them on at home, I decided I didn't like them. I said to myself, 'I'm going to get my money back if it's the last thing I do;' and I worked myself up into a rage thinking about how they might not let me return those shoes. I walked into the store boiling mad, you could see it all over my face, and sure enough I got into a ferocious battle with the manager, and to this day, I'll never set foot in that place again."

Maddy is beginning to understand the dynamics of her anger, that most of it is "old" leftover anger from her childhood, that she's been carrying a huge bag of it with her since her earliest years, that in order to relieve herself of some of the burden, make herself feel better, she has to engineer circumstances that allow her to vent small amounts of it at a time. The episode with her husband and the one at the shoe store are typical of the way she operates. She doesn't enjoy being a Creator, but she does need and enjoy releasing her feelings. Now she's working on alternative ways to handle her anger.

Are You a Creator?

Many Creators don't know why they express anger as they do. Stumbling in and out of the emotion for no apparent reason, they're a puzzle to themselves and to everyone else as well. If you can't make any sense out of the way you handle your anger, if you find yourself making waves when life is otherwise relatively quiet, if you have one or two regular scapegoats, people you consistently make the butt of your anger, or if you frequently lash out at "innocent" and unsuspecting strangers, you are a Creator.

What are you going to do about it? It's up to you, of course. You create for a reason: it gives you relief. You may also value the sense of power you obtain when you create. (Creators, because of their strong and direct use of anger, often assume a take-charge position in a group.) Keep in mind, however, that creating also tends to breed fear and mistrust in others. If your need for power and the feeling of being in charge is stronger than your need for warmth and closeness, then you may decide to go right on behaving as you do.

(Just remember that creating isn't the *only* way to get relief from angry tension. Neither is it the only way to have influence over others; indeed, real power is hardly ever exercised through mere "bullying.")

On the other hand, if you're not satisfied with creating as a way of life, if you think it interferes with your relationships, if you feel controlled by your anger rather than the other way around, you may want to experiment with other ways of dealing with the emotion. The following exercises should be helpful:

1. Reduce the persistent angry muscular tension in your body by getting lots of physical exercise. Running is excellent. If you can't get out to the park for a daily jog, or if you feel slightly foolish running around the block, then run in place for a minute or two several times a day. Stretching is good, too. So is deliberately tensing and then just as deliberately untensing the muscles in various parts of your body. If you can put your body at ease, you'll be better able to make conscious decisions.

2. *Breathe* your anger. Open your mouth wide and let your jaw hang down loose. As you inhale, pull in your abdomen. Imagine that the air around you is saturated with anger and you're pulling it all into your body. Fill yourself to capacity. Hold for a count of ten. Now, exhale slowly. Empty yourself of all that heavy, anger-laden air. Do this ten times, twice a day. At the end of each breathing session, imagine yourself an empty bag, utterly emptied of anger at least for the moment.

3. If you have a scapegoat, make a conscious effort to stop unloading on him/her. (Direct your

anger at someone else if you must.) Now that you've stopped using your regular scapegoat, what *do* you do with the emotion?

4. Think back to the last time you were a Creator. On paper or in your mind, try to reconstruct the incident step by step. How did you manipulate the circumstances so that you could vent your feelings? At what point did you realize you were angry? What came first, the anger or the situation? What did you gain by creating anger? What did you lose? Can you think of other ways of managing the same situation? What would it have been like to "stuff" your anger? Make a joke? Talk out your feelings in a calm, objective way?

5. Make a list of all the advantages of being a Creator. Next, make a list of the disadvantages. Think about these lists.

6. Go through this book and choose a mode of expressing anger that appeals to you, then promise yourself that the next time you feel the impulse to create, you'll use this other mode instead. (What's important here is *thinking* about doing something else with your feelings; in time, you may be able to act on what you're thinking.)

I wouldn't go so far as to say that all Creators are "bullies," but certainly many of them display a tendency to unload their anger onto those who are either literally or figuratively smaller and/or weaker than they are—on a child, for example, or on a vulnerable grown-up who has neither the strength nor the inclination to fight back. (Creators who are also employers or bosses can have a real field day with their anger, since their subordinates are naturally hesitant to stand up to them.) In fact, the Creator often has a talent for sniffing out weakness in others and, like Diane's father, once he's found himself a scapegoat he's understandably reluctant to let go of his prize.

However, the Creator doesn't always confine his anger to one or two scapegoats, but may attack almost anyone at any time, usually without warning. It is this very unpredictability that makes his anger so difficult for others to handle.

The Daydreamer

"I replay my anger over and over again in my head ... only I say and do things in my imagination that I never, ever could in real life."

A Daydreamer

"When I'm angry, I fantasize, think up punishments, ways to get even. In my fantasies, I'm very powerful and ruthless ... People respect me."

Another Daydreamer

In fantasy, the timid can be bold and aggressive, the weak are strong, the clumsy are full of grace, the tongue-tied discover vast verbal resources. In the privacy of the mind, we can all rise up in righteous wrath, and vengeance is ours.

So what's wrong with that? Very often, nothing at all. Those elaborate get-even scenarios constructed in our daydreams can help us get rid of anger we might not be able to unload otherwise.

Most of us are Daydreamers at least part of the time, because most of us—no, all of us—are less than perfect. We can't always handle real-life situations with the strength, the courage, the spunk, the cleverness we'd like to claim for ourselves. When we fall very far short of the mark in actuality, we can always make up for it in fantasy.

John, a tall, very lean man in his late thirties is a good example of the Daydreamer. A salesman, John has cultivated a sincere, affable manner because he says, "It's important to get the customer to trust you. Nobody wants to buy anything from an overly aggressive guy who delivers an all-purpose sales pitch, who doesn't relate on a friendly one-to-one basis." But while John truly believes that he's on the right track with his nice-guy approach, he also finds that some potential customers take advantage of the easygoing good-natured personality he projects.

"Maybe it's because I smile a lot and I don't pressure them . . . I don't know. Anyway, sometimes some of them play games with me. They want me to knock the price way down, or they ask for special concessions as a personal favor. Or they take a long time to make up their minds and then when they give me the go-ahead to write up the contract, they change their minds all of a sudden and decide not to buy.

"I want to blow my stack. I want to curse them out for wasting my time, smash their faces, pick them up and throw them out the showroom door. But of course I can't do any of these things because . . . well, I just can't. It wouldn't be smart. I can't even frown or mutter under my breath or anything because maybe they'll change their minds again and decide to buy after all. So I just smile and act gracious and understanding and tell them I've enjoyed meeting them anyway . . . it's been a pleasure . . . and, oh hell, this part of the business really stinks.

"So what I do is this. I go back to my little office

and close the door, put my feet up on the desk and think about what happened. But in my head, I change things around. I make it so that the customer is begging me to write up the order, but I won't close the deal. I tell him I won't take his dirty money because I don't sell to scum. I have standards and he's not good enough to buy from me, he'll have to go somewhere else. He doesn't know what hit him. He just stands there and finally he leaves in a daze.

"I feel a whole lot better afterward, and I can go out and meet the next customer without hating him on sight. Maybe my way is crazy, but it helps."

Crazy? Not a bit. On the contrary, John's daydreaming serves a very useful purpose. It allows him to discharge anger-energy in a safe, nondestructive way. If he were to act on his impulses and actually take a poke at a customer, he'd land in jail or at the very least, lose his job. John is in touch with reality and he knows this; he doesn't want either to happen, so instead he uses up all that angry energy in recreating situations in his head. The little stories he tells himself all have happy endings. In them, he is the winner. He emerges from them feeling vindicated. It really doesn't matter that he made it all up. He gets relief anyway.

John is a Daydreamer who recognizes his own anger; he feels it coursing through his body and he wants to do something about it, but he chooses to deal with it indirectly, through fantasy. If he were a different kind of person or, to put it more precisely, if his early anger experiences were somewhat different, he might choose to work out his feelings by doing something physical (as a matter of fact, one could categorize Daydreaming as a form of low-intensity Doing). But, perhaps because he was raised to keep his mouth shut and to refrain from any outright physical expressions of anger, while at the same time no constraints were placed upon his imagination, it's easiest for him to fantasize.

This last may be the major difference between Daydreamers and Doers. Daydreamers, at least the ones who handle their anger as John does (there are other kinds of Daydreamers, but we'll get to them later), feel very little if any guilt about harboring angry thoughts. For them, the emotion isn't necessarily bad and they don't hate themselves for it as some other anger-types, most notably the Corner People, do. But they grow up with the feeling that to express that anger outright, to admit it to anyone but themselves, would be risky. So instead they sit back and run those anger movies in their heads. Many Doers, on the other hand, are distinctly uncomfortable thinking angry thoughts, but are perfectly at ease about expressing the emotion in indirect, physical ways.

Most people are part-time Daydreamers, and that's fine. It's a relatively safe and harmless way to get rid of excess anger-energy, and the revenge element can make it downright pleasurable as well.

For example, Kathy, a twenty-two-year-old fledgling journalist, told me about how daydreaming helped her to handle the anger and resentment she felt when she found out that the young man she was living with and "semi-engaged to" intended to leave her in order to be with a close friend of hers.

"I always knew he found Alice attractive. I also

knew that Alice liked him a lot. When two people are drawn to one another . . . well . . . there's not much anyone can do about it. I mean it seemed pointless to me to come right out and tell either one of them that I was angry and thought I'd been badly treated. It certainly wouldn't have changed anything. So instead of throwing a fit and playing the role of the wronged woman, the 'hell hath no fury' bit, I simply turned my back on them both. I avoided them and I still do.

"But for a long while, every night in my bed before I went to sleep, I'd spin the most gorgeous fantasies about how some day they'd both be sorry. Like, he'd wake up one day with her and realize he'd made a terrible mistake, that it was really me, me, me he loved, and he'd come to see me, practically get down on his knees, begging me to take him back. But, and here's the good part, I'd tell him, 'No, it's too late. I've found someone else.' Another fantasy was that I'd be with this really fantastic guy, and Alice would make a grandstand play for him and he'd look at her and turn her down flat, and then the new guy and I would go off and discuss 'poor Alice,' and he'd shake his head and say 'She must be crazy to think I'd leave a wonderful, beautiful, smart girl like you for her.' "

Upon concluding the recounting of her fantasies, Kathy beamed and said, "Oh, I know, I know. That kind of thing is wishful thinking, but without it I think I would have cracked up. Now, it's six months later. I'm through with the fantasy, I don't need it anymore."

Like John, Kathy is in touch with her anger, and by playing it out in her imagination she gets relief. Other Daydreamers have far less control.

They're puzzled and disturbed by their fantasies, unaware that anger is the basis for the sometimes frightening images that come crowding into their heads.

"Why do I have these horrible, ugly thoughts?" a twenty-eight-year-old woman asked. "Why can't I get rid of them?" This woman (I'll call her Martha) was "visited" by frequent, recurring images of her child's dead body being removed from the twisted wreckage of a car, being hauled up from the bottom of a swimming pool, discovered in the charred remains of a fire, or strangled by the sheets of his own bed.

These catastrophic images were extremely unsettling to Martha. Even more upsetting than the images themselves, she said, was that they welled up from within her own mind, that these were her thoughts, and that try as she would, she couldn't stop herself from thinking them.

I asked Martha how she felt about being a mother. "I love my child," was the answer. I tried to explain to her that it is quite possible to love one's child and at the same time to be uncomfortable with the duties and responsibilities of parenthood, that you can even love your child and be simultaneously angry at him. "Impossible," she insisted. "How could anyone feel that kind of anger at an adorable, helpless two-year-old? It isn't anger. I'm either a monster or crazy, but it isn't anger." (How interesting, I remember thinking, that anger is so foul an emotion for some people that insanity or "monstrousness" are preferable.)

Some months later, however, Martha was able to admit that she *was* angry. "But not at my son," she said. "He couldn't help being born, it wasn't his fault.

"But what can I do?"—and here she broke down into tears—"I simply can't stand being cooped up in the house with him day after day after day, cleaning up his messes, listening to his whining, never having a spare minute to myself, being his maid, his servant, his slave . . ."

I told Martha that as a mother I was very well acquainted with that trapped feeling and that, of course, she was angry at her son, why shouldn't she be? Slaves are always angry at their masters.

With that, she brightened. "I guess I'll have to stop being a slave." Martha was lucky. She was able to find a part-time job that got her out of the house three days a week. She made barely enough to pay for a babysitter but for Martha, earning money was far less important than getting away from the house and out from under her son's thumb. She feels she and the boy have a better relationship now; those "horrible, ugly," angry thoughts are subsiding as Martha looks at them for what they are—anger in disguise.

People like Martha, who are plagued with strange, seemingly uncontrollable fantasies, are called "compulsives." What's up with the compulsive? How is his or her anger converted into disturbing images that refuse to go away?

To begin with, the compulsive Daydreamer is still another casualty of unacknowledged anger. He or she is usually angry at a loved one, most often someone very close (a child, a spouse, a parent). But the compulsive can't bear to admit that anger (which, incidentally, needn't be very intense; just a little bit, squelched over and over again, will do it). So, instead of saying to himself or herself, "I'm angry at X," and then obtaining release through fantasy, as the ordinary Daydreamer does, the compulsive leaves out the anger part and is left with only those punishing, vengeful images. (We could almost say that the compulsive is an ordinary Daydreamer, *minus* the *consciousness* of anger.) The images are so puzzling and frightening because they seem to come from nowhere and for no reason.

When the compulsive discovers the source of these obsessive fantasies, when a connection is made between them and anger, the fantasies often either fade or become manageable and subject to the Daydreamer's control.

For another kind of Daydreamer, the Escapist, fantasy is not so much a healthy release as it is an avoidance tactic. It would be incorrect to say that daydreaming doesn't help these people cope with their anger. It does. But it also allows them to maintain the illusion that certain problems are resolved, or needn't be dealt with in reality, because they've been worked out in fantasy. Let me give you an example:

On the surface, Bill is the most relaxed of men. At thirty-five, he has a well-paying job with a large insurance company. His work is highly valued and so is his ability to deal with people. His earthy warmth and humor have made him a favorite of the organization's stock boys and secretaries as well as its senior executives. They'd all be surprised to know that the mind of this charming, well-liked person is always busy churning violent anger fantasies.

The fact of the matter is that Bill hates his job. His real love is teaching and he feels he has a gift for it. But several years ago, because of a financial crisis that has long since past, he left his job as an instructor in the math department of a small junior college in order to take up his present, much-better paying position. His anger and frustration continue to grow, and at least once a month he composes a letter of resignation, but he never submits it because, in his own words, "it would be so hard to switch to a less affluent lifestyle," and because (my words now) his daydreams take the pressure off and thus enable him to avoid confronting his problem!

Greta is another Escapist. A brilliant young woman who nevertheless did poorly in college, she gets the message from her parents that they feel she's doomed to failure, that she'd be better off marrying the first man who asks her rather than pursue her dream of becoming a newspaper reporter. She's angry at them because of their lack of faith in her ability. But rather than use that anger-energy to achieve her goal in real life, she allows it to dribble away in get-even fantasies, where her parents humbly beg her pardon for underrating her talents. Daydreaming sometimes functions far *too* well as an anger-relieving device.

Most of us are capable of recognizing when it makes good sense to grin and bear it, turn the other cheek, etc. If you're a Daydreamer and you know when to keep your mouth shut and save your anger for a time when you can replay it, with a vengeance, in the privacy of your mind, and if you're also able to unleash your anger-energy when it can do you some good, then you're probably dealing very well indeed with angry feelings.

Fantasy is definitely one of the better ways to cope with anger that can't be expressed more openly, but getting into a daydreaming rut is just as wasteful and self-defeating as being locked into any other kind of rut.

A chronic Daydreamer who never handled anger in any other way is almost always an Escapist. There are worse things to be, I suppose, but the Escapist who attempts to fantasize *all* problems out of existence is missing out on an awful lot of what makes life worth living. Confronting problems and, hopefully, resolving them adds enormously to one's sense of competency and self-esteem; in fact, the feeling of being whole, alive, and fully functioning depends on it.

If you're an Escapist, remember that while daydreaming can help you get rid of pent-up anger, it won't solve your problems (unless, of course, you take up permanent residence in fantasyland . . . but that's an altogether different story). Only confrontation does that. With this in mind, perhaps you will want to explore the possibility of expressing your feelings in other, more direct ways.

Are You a Daydreamer?

1. The very next time you slip off into a daydream, stop. Come back to reality. Ask yourself *why* you're angry. Once you're clear about the reason for your feelings, the "problem," try to decide whether daydreaming really is an appropriate way to handle it. If, for example, you're angry about something someone else has said or done, is there any good reason not to let that person know how you feel? The answer to this one might very well be "yes" (there *are* situations where a direct expression of anger can only make things worse and it would be foolish to deny it). In which case, day-

dreams are appropriate and will give you the release from angry tension that you seek. But what if the answer is "no"? What if you're hopping mad because your spouse forgot your birthday, for example, or the guy next door *still* hasn't returned the power mower you lent him last spring? Why not *say* something about it, instead of spending precious time and energy (mentally) making that person whine for mercy?

Speaking out gets your message across and lets others know how you feel; daydreaming doesn't. Speaking out may get you what you want; daydreaming can't.

2. If most of your daydreams revolve around ongoing situations, a job you don't like, for example, or a relationship that causes you pain, try to sharpen the focus of those fantasies. Eliminate the grotesque, the impossible, and the highly unlikely, and bring your daydreams more into line with reality. In other words, don't stop thinking about those troubling situations, but do start thinking about them with the idea of discovering new ways to deal with them in the real world.

Ned, a teen-ager, comes to mind here. Ned spent a lot of time daydreaming about outdoing his older brother who is, according to Ned, "good at everything." Ned was angry because he felt he always had been and always would be secondary to his brother, not only in the eyes of his parents, but to everyone else as well. (Whether the parents and other people in Ned's life really did favor the older brother is not as important as the fact that Ned felt that way.)

I encouraged Ned to continue daydreaming but to be more specific and realistic about it, to focus on fantasies that contained an element of the possible. He was unsure about how to do this, so I asked him whether he felt he did anything well. The answer was no. Then I queried him about his interests. He said he "sort of liked" taking pictures. I urged him to start fantasizing about how good he would feel if he developed his ability as a photographer. He did, and eventually bought a new camera. At the moment, Ned is investing some of the energy generated by his anger in learning to take better and better pictures. He still fantasizes about outdoing his brother, but he feels better about himself, less hopeless, less put down, more able to do and be what he wants.

The Doer

"I find that when I'm in a bad mood, my tennis game improves ... I can really murder that ball."

A Doer

"The worse I feel, the more I want to get out and move around. Whatever is bothering me, I know I can sort of tune it out, forget about it, by doing something strenuous."

Another Doer

In a sense, the Doer is the opposite of the Body Person: whereas the Body Person uses his physical self as a closed receptacle for anger-energy (and thereby brings on any of a number of psychosomatic ailments), the Doer's body acts as an open-ended conductor of anger, and instead of accumulating, the energy gets *used*. Doers are not always perfect examples of good health and right living, but nevertheless we would all probably be better off, both physically and emotionally, if we could be Doers at least some of the time.

In fact, some of the "new" therapies derive from what the natural-born Doer always knew in his very bones: that physical activity is a good, healthy way to get rid of the poisons of accumulated anger.

Encounter-group techniques are based on doing as a way of unloading anger. In a heated-up emotional atmosphere, participants are encouraged (indeed, sometimes goaded and harassed) to stand up in front of the group and to shout, curse, and cry their way through to the other side of their anger.

It works. But now that the encounter-group movement is a little older and maybe a little wiser, the therapists have found that while the initial relief of reliving one's anger (which is the purpose of all that shouting, cursing, and crying) is tremendous, like having a huge bowel movement, as someone once said, the "results" are not permanent. Or at least not unless the "doing" is accompanied by some new insight and understanding.

Arthur Janov, the originator of *primal scream therapy,* believes that we all carry with us the remnants of "primal" anger, expressed as bodily tension, which began when we were infants, before we knew how to verbalize, when all we could do with our anger was to lie impotent in our cribs, crying out our discontent, our bodies stiff and rigid with frustration. Janov says that the only way to relieve this tension is to somehow recapture that original feeling of impotent rage, which we could never fully express as infants because of the fear of losing parental love, and then to scream out our anguish and anger. According to Janov, if and when we are able to go back to the scene of the crime (not *our* crime, but our parents' crimes against our helplessness) and achieve that primal scream, years' worth of anger-energy and tension will be dissipated.

Reichian therapy, too, is predicated on the concept that tension and anger are rooted in the body and must be released by "doing" (only in this case, the therapist does the doing).

While *traditional Freudian* therapy held that feelings of frustration and anger would be eased if the patient could only *talk* about them, these other therapies were developed out of the realization that though verbalization helped many patients to gain an *intellectual* understanding of their problems, they nevertheless continued to experience the emotional stress and bodily tension associated with pent-up anger.

Rolfing, a form of massage, is still another one of these tension-relieving techniques. The patient lies on a massage table, while a specially trained therapist proceeds to apply the full weight of his body to the patient at various pressure points. Step by step, the therapist works on first one, then another area, and far from its being a pleasant, relaxing experience, this treatment actually hurts.

The idea is that after a number of strenuous, painful sessions, the body is somehow changed. The patient will stand taller and more erect than ever before, his movements will be freer, and the tension that has been locked into the muscles since early childhood will be released. According to exponents of this kind of massage therapy, long-lost hidden memories come flooding back when certain muscles are manipulated. It is not an easy therapy, and as I mentioned before, it hurts. But those who've undergone it claim that there is indeed a kind of pleasure derived from the pain.

At some point in the future, body therapy may be all in a day's work. Even now, at some large Japanese factories, there is an anger room on the premises, a special room where employees may go to during the Japanese equivalent of a coffee break. There is a large photograph of the owner of the factory in this room, and a set of darts. The employees can release some of the tension, resentment, and hostility they feel at having to be there eight long, boring hours a day, performing dull, repetitive jobs, by deliberately striking out at the image of the person who is "the boss."

It's the rare office or factory where feelings of anger and resentment don't build, at least occasionally, to the point where they become a choking, almost palpable presence that affects the work that gets done, reducing it to a minimum. I haven't seen any figures on how those Japanese anger rooms have influenced the levels of production and job satisfaction or the rate of worker absenteeism, but undoubtedly management, in recognizing and trying to alleviate employee frustration in this way, is taking a step in the right direction.

As we can see, it isn't only the individual Doer who realizes that body work, exercise, activity, motion, is a fine way to handle anger. Whole therapies are growing up around the concept, and the idea is being adapted even by the business sector.

Of all the different modes of anger-release, "doing" may be the healthiest. But only when the individual is aware of what's happening when he or she does. There's a big difference between burying one's anger in activity which may amount to escapism, and acknowledging one's anger and then deliberately setting out to work it off through physical activity. In other words, as the encounter-group people are finding out, if the relief of doing is going to be lasting and meaningful, you've got to at least try to figure out what's bugging you in the first place.

Sexual athletes, for example, those people who "do" in bed, may *say* they need the release of intercourse a couple of times a day (or more often in some cases) in order to feel comfortable, or as one man said, "because I'm so horny." Well, I can't help feeling a little bit suspicious when I hear something like this, and I always wonder, is it because the person is really so very horny, or is sexual aggressiveness actually a way of working out anger directed at the partner? Many times it's the latter.

In the same way, many men and women who consistently overwork themselves when there is no very pressing financial reason for it are not so much devoted to their jobs as they are compelled by the need to rid themselves of large amounts of residual anger, which isn't all bad. Each of us has a perfect right to spend our time as we wish, and working is as good a way as any. If we're going to overwork, however, we should be aware of the possible consequences of diverting so much time and energy away from spouse, children, and other personal and social obligations and pleasures. We should also ask ourselves about that anger.

For some people, doing amounts to little more than reflex action, busy-work. Their doing is undirected. There's no rhyme or reason to it. These

people often are the kind who find it next to impossible to sit still for any length of time and they
attribute it, falsely for the most part, to having an
overabundance of "nervous energy."

I'm thinking of Patricia, a forty-five-year-old
woman I know who is constantly on the move. She
plays both tennis and golf twice a week, which,
she admitted, is more often than she really cares
to, runs around in the car on errands that don't
need doing, dusts, polishes, waxes, and scrubs the
surfaces of her already sparkling house "just to
keep busy," and collapses into bed each night with
the feeling that still another day in her life has
been wasted.

I asked her what she was so angry about. She
blinked once or twice. "I don't get it," she said. "I
didn't say anything about being angry."

"No, you didn't," I conceded. "But just for the
moment, let's assume that you are angry, only you
don't know it. What's happening in your life that
you don't feel good about?"

"Well, that's another story," she said. "I don't
feel good about staying home alone for weeks at a
time when my husband goes off on business trips.
I don't feel good about his insisting that his
mother come to live with us. I don't feel good
about his losing sexual interest in me, and yes,
you're right, I *am* angry. At him."

I wish I could report that having discovered her
angry feelings, Patricia was able to go home that
afternoon and work everything out with her husband, but it didn't happen that way. He still goes
off on long business trips, though he's planning to
take her with him on the next one; their sexual
encounters are still infrequent and uninspired; he
still wants his mother to come live with them; and

Patricia still unloads some of her anger by playing tennis and golf, running errands, and cleaning the house. There's a difference, though: Patricia *knows* that she's angry now, and she also knows why. And while these discoveries didn't exactly solve her problems, at least she understands what she has to deal with.

In contrast to Patricia, a Doer who was unaware of why she "did," other Doers are very much in touch with their feelings and have developed some rather ingenious ways of getting anger up and out of their systems.

There is the harried executive, for example, who can almost feel his blood pressure mounting during some particularly trying business meeting, but who elects to keep his mouth shut and his opinions to himself all the same. When the meeting is over, he fumes back to his office, closes the door and jogs in place for ten minutes or so, after which he emerges, calm and smiling, his anger-energy dissipated by those few minutes of activity.

Another conscious Doer, a writer, is always filled with both anxiety and anger from the moment she sends a completed manuscript off to her publisher until she has word of its acceptance (or rejection). During this time, which might range anywhere from a week to a month, she gets out her sewing machine and makes clothes for herself and her two daughters. "The funny thing is," she told me, "I sew very badly. I hardly ever wear anything I make and neither do the girls. It's going through the motions, you know, cutting the fabric, pinning, basting, working at the machine, that counts."

Whenever John, a real estate salesman and Doer, felt the tension of anger coiling more tightly within him, he'd go outside and weed the acre of lawn surrounding his suburban house. Each and every week, he told me, represented anger pulled out by its roots. Just recently he moved to an apartment in the city and he desperately misses his lawn and his special anger technique. Now he's forced to go and work out his anger-energy at the "Y" "which is better than nothing," he says. "Still, basketball, swimming, punching a bag ... all that stuff ... it's just not the same as plucking out those damn weeds."

How does the Doer get that way in the first place? Or, to be more precise, why do some people reach adulthood knowing how to do away with their anger as a matter of course, while others take to totally different modes of handling the emotion? No one knows for sure, of course, why *anybody* does *anything* one way rather than another, but my feeling is that the Doer as a growing child was subjected to environmental influences that encouraged him to retain his "physicality." ("Physicality," as I use the word here, has less to do with athletic ability than it does with a certain heightened sense of awareness and enjoyment of the body; "physical" people get more mileage from their bodies, though they are not necessarily any stronger, more agile, or better coordinated than others.) Most of us were *born* physical. (Watch an infant or very small child, and you'll see what I mean. Whatever the young individual does, both mind and body are totally and equally involved.) Later on, our physicality was more or less inhibited, depending on how and where we lived, our parents' attitudes about our bodies and their own, the way we chose (or were forced) to spend our time, and, of course, our own innate propensities for being active or passive, sense-oriented or abstract-thought oriented, etc. When physicality is greatly stifled, as it is with many whose parents placed a very high value on intellectuality—there is a tendency to "lose touch" with the body and to "feel" as well as express emotion with the "head" or "mind" only. Very often we hear someone say that emotions—sadness, happiness, anger—are states of mind, which is not entirely false. But they are also "states of body." With grief, our postures droop, our faces sag; with happiness, our expressions brighten, our steps are buoyant; with anger, our muscles grow tense, anticipating action.

Unlike some other anger-types then, Doers have retained some sense of original body/mind unity. They either can't or won't confine emotion to the "head," perhaps because as children their physicality was valued; at the very least, it was tolerated.

It's unfortunate that so many city children and some suburban and country kids, too, are allowed to sit for hours in front of their TV sets. They need more *doing,* more healthy outlets for their energy, more exercise, not just for the benefit of their growing bodies, but for their emotional well-being as well. It seems to me that parents who allow or encourage physical passivity in their children are doing them a disservice. So are those mothers and fathers who transmit the message that "heads count, bodies don't." Young minds and bodies as well as older ones need physical action for tension release.

I'll be interested to see how the children of one enlightened young couple I know handle their anger when they grow up. These parents have provided an "anger corner," equipped with punching bag, old rag dolls, and broken toys. The children can go there when they're feeling frustrated and punch (but not each other), throw, rip, tear, and break until the anger is drained away from their small bodies. These kids are also permitted to express their feelings verbally and directly to their parents and siblings. Maybe they won't all grow up to be Doers, but it's highly unlikely that any of them will become Body People, Corner People, or go the route to Stufferdom (see page 134).

Are You a Doer?

If you're a Doer, you're aware, either consciously or on an instinctive level, that anger isn't just something that arises and stays in the head, but is instead a kind of energy that pervades the whole self, mind and body. You want, no, need, to use that energy. So you jog, swim, garden, sew, clean, punch, or otherwise do away with your anger.

As a Doer, you can rid yourself of that anger relatively quickly and easily. You aren't a sulker, a seether, an Actor who runs the risk of frightening others with dramatic scenes, or a Big Talker whose endless verbalizations may bore, annoy, or ultimately hurt the people closest to you. As a Doer, in fact, you may be a master at what is possibly the best and healthiest way to handle anger.

But just for a moment, let's consider your personal mode of doing.

If you're a Doer by choice, you probably do only most, or some, of the time. In other words, you know when and why you're angry and you choose to deal with the feeling by going out and chopping firewood (or whatever) when it seems appropriate to the circumstances. At other times you choose some other way of expressing yourself (Perhaps you switch to big talking or acting. Perhaps you play the Comedian, dispelling tension with humor.) Doing is your primary technique, but you have more than one way of responding to frustration and so you're in no danger of falling into an anger rut you can't get out of.

On the other hand, you may be a mindless Doer like Patricia, driven by a vague sense of restlessness and unease. You're tense and physical activity dispels some of your tension. But what's that tension all about? Who, or what, is making you angry?

1. One way to find out is to ask yourself the same question I asked Patricia: What's happening in your life that you don't feel good about? It's always a good idea to sit down with paper and pencil and jot down your responses to this question. If nothing comes to mind immediately, try again a few days from now. Once you've got a fix on what's bothering you, you'll be in a better position to decide whether to continue to cope by doing more or to take a more direct approach instead.

The Saboteur

"I'm very rarely angry at anybody . . . yet, it seems like I'm always mixed up in a situation where someone's down on *me*."

A Saboteur

The poor soul quoted above, let's call him Mark, feels like a victim. He says he doesn't understand why people are always angry at him. Oh, sure, he realizes that they don't like it when he's late. And he admits it: he *is* late, sometimes *very* late, for most appointments. *But he can't help it.* "Something always comes up," he says. However, they (the people waiting for him) just can't get it through their heads that he's not to blame.

Let's take a closer look at Mark. He's part of a regular Saturday golf foursome. He and the other three, all of them men who work at Mark's office, have been playing together for almost two years now. With very rare exceptions, Joe, Benny, and Chuck manage to get to the links by 7:30 A.M. Then, again with rare exceptions, they have to stand around waiting for Mark for forty-five minutes or so (once it was two hours) . When Mark finally does show up, he's full of apologies. And excuses. The apologies are spoken with sincerity and the excuses at least *sound* valid (the clock was slow or the alarm didn't go off, his wife picked a fight, the car wouldn't start, he got halfway out to the golf club and then had to backtrack because he'd forgotten his shoes . . . that sort of thing). And he always promises it won't happen again. But it always does.

The other three actually got together at work one day to discuss what to do about this annoying state of affairs. They finally decided that on the following Saturday, instead of waiting for Mark, they would go on without him. Assuming he was late again, they'd give him the silent treatment when he finally caught up with them on the course. So that's what they did.

This tactic didn't work. Mark continued to be late and the others realized that there probably was very little they could do to change his behavior;

rather, they would have to choose between either not playing with him at all or accepting him as he was. Joe and Benny voted not to exclude Mark (of the four, he was the best golfer and frequently gave the others tips on how to improve their putting techniques, etc.). Chuck was fed up with Mark and didn't want to bother with him anymore, but he went along with the other two. However, at Chuck's suggestions, it was decided to throw a scare into Mark and *threaten* to oust him from the group if he didn't mend his ways.

Upon receiving this bit of information, Mark made it his business to be no more than ten minutes late for the next three sessions. But then the backsliding began, and soon he was as tardy as ever.

Joe is a perceptive man who recognizes that Mark's lateness is a way of saying "Hey, you guys, I'll show you. You think you're big shots, but I can be an even bigger shot by making you angry." I go along with Joe's interpretation. There's no doubt that anger is the basis for Mark's lateness. He has all the earmarks of the Saboteur.

If we could creep inside the Saboteur's mind to examine its special kind of anger dynamics, we'd discover a big, fat mental block preventing the individual from directly experiencing the emotion. The anger is there, but because it isn't *felt* as anger, it isn't expressed as anger—or at least not the kind of verbal or physical behavior we ordinarily associate with the word. As we've seen, many people are cut off from their angry feelings, which are therefore manifested in peculiar, often self-destructive ways—as, for example, the physical ailments of the Body Person, the depression and self-hate of the Corner Person, the overeating of the Stuffer, etc., and etc. The Saboteur expresses anger in an equally odd way: he becomes a chronic forgetter, loser, breaker (or spiller or burner); or, like Mark, he is always late.

By forgetting, losing, "accidentally" destroying someone else's property or always being late, the Saboteur is able to make others suffer without experiencing the discomfort of being held responsible for these angry acts. At worst, he gets a reputation for being careless or thoughtless (or, if the Saboteur is a woman, she might be called "dizzy" or "flighty"). Anyone who isn't acquainted with the dynamics of anger and the many forms it may take may deny the connection between this kind of behavior and hostility. (After all, who *doesn't* occasionally forget an appointment? Who *hasn't* been legitimately and unavoidably delayed from time to time?) The real question is, how frequently does it happen?

On first consideration, it appears that the Saboteur has it made. Since most people know what it means to "slip up" on occasion, the Saboteur can commit his petty meannesses and—assuming he dons the proper air of contrition afterward—the people he has inconvenienced are usually willing to make allowances and forgive him. He gets away with it. For a while, anyway.

Except that his behavior is chronic. He *often* forgets to be where he says he's going to be and do what he says he's going to do. He habitually loses things (especially other people's possessions). You can almost count on him to break something ("accidentally" of course) when he comes to visit. And he's always late.

Eventually, the people who know him best get wise. They begin to resent his forgetfulness, his

thoughtlessness. They either call him on his behavior or disassociate themselves from him. *They*
become angry.

At which point, the Saboteur feels victimized
and misunderstood (can *I* help it if I happen to be
the kind of person who has trouble remembering
things? Is it *my* fault?). At the same time, he gets
perverted pleasure at being the focus of all that
angry attention (they're noticing me! I'm important! I can make them angry!).

Like most of us, the Saboteur is really getting
back at Mommy and Daddy, who probably didn't
pay much attention to him as a child. Being ignored made him angry, but he couldn't express
that anger directly because if he did, they might
punish him by withdrawing even further, and
then he'd be in a fine fix. So instead he dawdled
and lost things and had accidents and couldn't
remember, just like the grown-up Saboteur he
was destined to become. Mommy and Daddy were
chagrined, but at least they didn't punish him because they didn't believe he was that way by
choice; it was simply his "nature."

As one might expect, the Saboteur vehemently
rejects any suggestion that his forgetfulness (carelessness, lateness, or whatever) is actually hostility
in disguise. "But I don't *feel* angry," is the usual
retort. And indeed, it's doubtful that he has any
conscious awareness of anger.

A young man I know told me about his Saboteur mother who could accept the link between
her behavior and her anger only after months of
therapy. During all the time he was growing up,
this young man remembers very few occasions
when dinner, or at least part of it (usually the
meat), didn't arrive at the table charred to taste-

lessness. His mother, he said, was always apologetic, always had some plausible excuse, like the telephone ringing, or someone coming to the door, or a minor crisis in another part of the house that caused her to "forget" whatever was cooking on the stove.

It's hard to believe that this could have gone on for so many years without somebody, the husband, the children, the wife herself, questioning what was really happening. But apparently, *that's the way it was*. Yes, of course, the other members of the family were annoyed. Yes, of course, they frequently expressed their anger. But mostly they tolerated their burned dinners because, well, "That's just Mom's way, she isn't a great cook, and what can you do about it." After a while it even became something of a family joke.

The son remembers that otherwise she was a "sweet" and even-tempered woman, always bowing to her husband's wishes, always picking up after him and the children, never demanding much of anything from anybody for herself. It was only in the matter of feeding her family (and isn't the giving of food a gesture of love?) that she was able to express her frustration, to say, not in so many words but in an even more dramatic, acting-out way: "Here. See this food? This is what you get because you deserve it and I don't like you and the way you treat me, and I'm sick of this miserable job."

When her husband decided to leave—*not* because of anything she had or hadn't done, he assured her, but because he'd found someone else who "understood" him better—this woman entered therapy. Her feelings at the time vacillated between utter devastation and intense relief. The devastation, she understood (she had married young, going directly from her father's care to her husband's; she didn't see how she could possibly survive without a man). But the sense of relief puzzled her. "I should feel miserable about the separation," she said, "and most of the time I do. But other times I feel . . . how shall I put it? . . . like I've had a tooth that was bothering me for ages, and now the tooth's been pulled." When it was suggested that perhaps she'd been angry at her husband for a long, long time, her denial was typical of the Saboteur: "If I were angry at anyone, I'd be the first one to know about it."

Several weeks went by, during which time the woman was encouraged to focus on feelings of anger, not as something bad, but as a kind of red alert that tells one all is not well, until one day she speculated to the therapist that possibly she *was* angry, possibly she *had* resented the way her husband had treated her ("full-time maid and part-time person" were her words) and that maybe one *could* be angry without being fully conscious of the feeling. "Strange," she mused at one point, "I used to be so lousy with food, but now that I'm cooking mostly for myself, I hardly ever burn anything anymore . . ."

Sabotage is a sneaky way to get one's anger message across. Not so much because the Saboteur is necessarily such a sneaky person, but because the anger is expressed so deviously and in such "small" ways. The Saboteur hangs you up, but his behavior rarely causes real anguish. It seems that even the most careless Saboteurs manage to keep their wits about them when the stakes are high, which indicates that their carelessness is *not* a matter over which they have *no* control. (One woman, for example, consistently forgot to pick up cigarettes for her husband when she went shopping, though he always reminded her as she left the house; but when guests were expected, she *always* remembered to buy several packs in case her visitors ran out of their own. A man, with a well-established reputation for lateness, always managed to get to the opera, which he adored, several minutes before curtain time.)

I would suspect anyone who habitually "forgets" small committments, i.e., a promise to do a favor for someone, an agreement to meet another person at a certain time and place, etc., as being a Saboteur.

In the same way, the person who has numerous "accidents," who frequently drops small, breakable objects, or spills soup, coffee, cocktails, or cigarette ashes where they do the most damage, may be expressing anger through sabotage. (These people usually apologize in a tone that says, "I'm sorry, but I can't help being 'all thumbs.'" However, if you know someone like this, it might be interesting to watch and see whether his clumsiness shows itself in his own house, with his own belongings.)

Chronic interrupting, where one person can't or won't allow anyone else to speak without cutting in and taking over the conversation, is another form of sabotage. (I suppose the classic example is the husband who always stops his wife in the middle of a story with a remark such as "You've got it all wrong, let me tell it," or "You left out the most important part.")

Another kind of Saboteur comes across as being somewhat "vague," or fuddled, or on occasion, downright stupid, though it's probably difficult to believe wholly in this person's "stupidity," because he or she may demonstrate undeniable competence and possibly brilliance in many other situations. What's up here? In the same way that the forgetter is so conveniently able to "forget" when it suits his angry purposes, the vague one turns off his mind, or part of it. His response to what you're saying is confused, uncomprehending, seemingly dull-witted, because he's not paying attention. Tuning you out is his way of telling you he's angry. (I remember informing a friend of mine that a mutual acquaintance, someone neither of us had seen in years, was back in town. My friend's response was a vacant stare. About a week later, my friend burst in, annoyed, saying "I just ran into Sheila. Why didn't you *tell* me you'd seen her?") Although one's initial reaction to the vague one may be puzzlement mixed with pity (poor soul . . . can't get the simplest thing through his head), with further contact it becomes evident that the vagueness is a putdown: you and your ideas and your words are so inconsequential to the vague one that they don't even merit an attempt at understanding.

Boredom is still another cover-up for hostility. I suppose there is such a thing as "legitimate" boredom (some people simply aren't all that interesting), but whenever anyone tells me that it's impossible to spend time with So-and-So, I have to conclude that underneath it all, the bored one harbors some kind of unconscious resentment toward the borer that he can't or won't express otherwise. When we call someone "boring," we're not only dismissing him for his dullness, we're saying by implication that he's not fit company for the likes of us. To *feel* bored and to show it by yawning, gazing off into space, acting preoccupied or in a hurry to go someplace else, is a form of sabotage that chips away at the other person's self-esteem. (Boredom at school or on the job, incidentally, is frequently connected with anger at having to be there in the first place.)

Finally, there is the Saboteur who misrepresents himself and/or his intentions, who manages to convey an emotion or feeling or point of view that is false. The first example that comes to mind is the sexual tease, who comes on strong, either physically or verbally, but only up to a point, and then beats a hasty retreat. The other person is left hanging there, suspended in midair, aroused and full of sexual tension but with no immediate hope of gratification. The Saboteur-tease may claim that he or she never meant to lead the other person on, that the other person simply misread the signals. Well . . . maybe. More likely, it was a deliberate though subconscious attempt on the part of the Saboteur to punish the other (either as an individual, or as a "representative" of one sex or the other).

We're all entitled to change our minds about anything at any time, and it's too bad if someone else suffers as a result. That's the way it has to be, once in a while. To do it habitually is another matter entirely. To raise false expectations, either sexually or in friendship, or at work or in any other sphere, and then to backtrack, leaving the other person feeling foolish, confused, disappointed, betrayed, is an act of hostility. Often, there is a direct or indirect expression of reciprocal anger. Which may be just what the Saboteur is after in the first place.

Are You a Saboteur?

If any of the foregoing rings a bell for you, you might be a Saboteur. You probably are one if, in addition to being aware of your own hangup(s), you get feedback about it from others, too. Some of the people in your life may have developed a tolerance to your behavior; they may even think enough of you to make their own adjustments to it. (If you're always late, your friends might take your tardiness into account, for example, by asking you to meet them at seven, when they themselves don't plan to be there until eight.) Others will simply be alienated and express their anger, and this may make you feel misunderstood. You want it known that you aren't *deliberately* late (or forgetful, or careless, or whatever); it's something you can't help.

As a Saboteur you *are* controlling your own behavior, only it's a kind of indirect, remote control emanating from someplace deep in your subconscious. You're late, forgetful, careless, etc., because you're angry at someone or something and it's the only way you're able to express it. If you want to stop hanging up other people (which always results in being a hangup to yourself), the first step is to try to discover why you're angry, and the second is to consider other ways of dealing with the emotion. The following exercise may be helpful:

1. Think back and try to remember the last time you played the Saboteur. Who was your victim? What are your feelings about him/her? (You may be in the habit of thinking about this person as a "friend" or even a "close friend." Try to get

beyond this and discover the true nature of the relationship. Who's the giver? Who's the taker? Who's more powerful? What needs of yours does this person fulfill? How do you suppose you satisfy his/her needs? Do you feel uneasy about him/her?)

Did this person excuse or ignore your act of sabotage? Or did he/she express anger? How did *you* feel about having played the Saboteur?

2. Whatever your particular brand of sabotage may be, try to imagine how you would feel about being on the receiving end of that behavior. Would it bother you? (If yes, why? And would you show it? If not, why not?)

3. Complete the following:

I am angry at _____ because _____.
Whose name came first into your mind? Have you ever sabotaged this person?

Now, make up a story in which you're angry, whole-body angry, with this person. How would you handle it? What method feels most comfortable? (If you can't think of anything offhand, skim through this book to find out what other people do with their anger.)

4. Practice feeling angry. Sit quietly, close your eyes, and imagine yourself surrounded by anger. Take a deep breath, pulling all that anger into your body. Then breathe out the same anger. Do this several times, thinking of someone, or something, that bothers you.

5. Do what you can to arrange your life so that it becomes more difficult to be a Saboteur. If you're always late, set your clock ahead by half an hour (or an hour!). If you're a forgetter, get yourself a date book and write in every single appointment and commitment as you make it. (This

means you'll have to carry it with you everywhere you go.) If your hostility takes the form of carelessness—spilling, dropping, burning, etc.—there isn't much you can do except to try to be more conscious of your actions. The same goes for not paying attention, indicating boredom, and misrepresenting yourself. Your anger needs to go *somewhere*. If you stop sabotaging, it may be easier for you to get rid of it in other ways. (Consider talking it out, doing, daydreaming, and humor as other possible outlets.)

The Sexed-Up Angry Couple

"The best sex is when we've had a fight and we make up in bed. But sometimes I think this isn't the way it *should* be . . ."

A wife

"It's not right to be so angry at someone you love . . ."

Another wife

"Lately, the fights are so bad, even the sex has gone sour . . ."

A husband

A good man-woman relationship thrives on good feelings, of course, and good times. Laughing, talking, walking hand-in-hand, singing, dancing, tenderness in and out of bed, a wanting to be together, a mutual effort to understand each other.

But one day, and that "one day" may come weeks, months, or even years after their first meeting, someone gets angry. Not just play-angry, lovers'-quarrel angry, but the real gut-exploding thing, and it's as if the ground has opened up between them and they look at each other as though for the first time and neither of them particularly likes what he or she sees.

"So, he's really a tyrant underneath it all."

"I never dreamed she could be so vicious."

It happens to many couples and it's not so terrible in itself. But if somebody doesn't do something—quick!—the bad feelings can build to the point that neither wants to risk opening up to the other again. The happiness and joy evaporate, and they begin to wonder if they wouldn't be better off apart.

How does it all happen? Does that first anger appear suddenly from out of the blue, a force of nature like a thunderstorm or a tidal wave, against which the two people are helpless to defend their relationship?

Well . . . yes, and no. Neither of them foresaw that first anger. It was inconceivable during the initial, happy, getting-to-know-you stage when they were everything to each other and each newly discovered flaw seemed adorable, a "perfect" flaw. No new anger was generated then and the old, unresolved anger that each of us collects from early childhood lay packed away, dormant. But it was there all right. And when some of the bright, shiny newness wore off and their eyes began to focus more clearly on each other, when they felt secure enough in the day-to-dayness of being together to drop their masks, their anger, which is as much a part of them (and us) as love, lay exposed and ready to be ignited. Eventually, there is a flare-up.

When a relationship is new, there's a tendency to take that anger and put it to bed. Literally. To say "Fuck you" to those bad feelings and get rid of them with sex.

Fuck you.

Have you ever said it? When you're angry? If you have, you didn't actually mean it in quite that way, right? What you were trying to get across was "Damn you, you're a pain in the neck, get out of my life," etc. So at first thought that phrase "Fuck you" seems an especially inappropriate way of expressing negative feeling. Sex is supposed to be good. And if it *is* good, why say "Fuck you" in anger? However, on second thought, it's not such a strange choice of words, after all.

Every one of us has a basic need, a drive, for sex. We also have this other drive, let's call it an "aggressive" instinct, and these two drives, sex and aggression, go hand in hand. Indeed, heterosexual intercourse, penis/vagina sex, *is* an act of aggression (the male organ as it enters the female, no matter how willing she may be, is actually invading her body). So are some of our other sexual behaviors. Certain kisses, where the tongue is thrust deeply into the lover's mouth, are aggressive. And what about those "love bites" that actually leave tooth marks and cause the partner to flinch or actually cry out in mixed pain and pleasure? What we used to call "hickies" and are actually small bruises left by overzealous sucking. And the long, raking scratches of the partner's fingernails? And the slaps, the pinches, the rib-crushing embraces? They are all *aggressive* expressions of love.

Children perceive the aggressive aspect of sex. Many a little boy or girl who sees Mommy and

Daddy having intercourse concludes that they are fighting (otherwise, why are they heaving their bodies like that?). That kids make the sex-aggression connection early in life is evidenced in many ways. When little boys torment little girls, pull their hair, frighten them with caterpillars, etc., they are obviously being aggressive. They are just as obviously being "sexy" as well.

Some grown-up sex is simply the hair-pulling antics of the seven-year-old brought up to date. Sometimes the little girl in the woman provokes the whole thing by angry flirting or taunting. ("Ha, ha, you can't catch me," or what amounts to the same thing, when really, being caught is the whole idea.) At which point he, figuratively or literally, chases her around the room. He then grabs her, the couple wrestle around a while and finally tear each other's clothes off. End of fight. The anger is resolved, at least for the moment. And the tension is dissipated by orgasm. No wonder that so many couples have discovered that sometimes the very best sex takes place just after a fight, when bodies are in high gear and emotional temperatures are well above the boiling point.

As for actual physical roughness, there's probably more of it when a couple makes up in bed than in their other sexual encounters, and this roughness may add to the unique excitement of angry sex. I'm not proposing either more brutality or less tenderness (this is a purely personal matter and depends on what pleases each partner most), but simply that since fighting and making-up and fighting and making-up seem to be part of the nature of things between a man and woman, why not accept it and enjoy it?

"I used to think that lovemaking had to be gentle, romantic, and soft," one woman told me. "But it hardly ever turned me on. One night Jerry and I had been fighting and we ended up in bed. I was still angry, and I bit his thigh. I'd never done anything like that before and he was astonished. He screamed, 'Oh, you *hurt* me,' but he loved it and then he did the same thing to me. When we climaxed, it was the biggest bang we'd had in ages. But something nagged at me later. Was there something wrong with me? Was I kookie or sadistic or something because I enjoyed rough sex?"

The answer if "No, of course not." As long as the mix of tenderness and aggression works for the two people involved, then there doesn't seem to be any reason not to enjoy it. If angry sex leads to bigger and better orgasms, all anyone can say is . . . why not?

The problem is, there's always a next time for anger, and a time after that, and still another time. And so on. If sex wipes the anger slate clean every single time, for both the man and the woman, then all well and good. However, more often than not, and even when the sex is sensational, there's a little bit of lingering, leftover anger. It sits there unresolved, and maybe the next time there's a fight followed by sex, that first bit of anger is joined by a little bit more. Sooner or later, those small individual piles of unresolved anger have grown huge and heavy, and rather than being a stimulus for good sex, the anger becomes a turn-off.

What happens then? Do words like "I'm sorry," and "I forgive you," and "It will never happen again" make the anger go away? For most couples most of the time, no. Even though each partner might like nothing better than to forgive and forget, those bags of anger chock full of carefully stored bad feelings and memories keep getting in the way. Old hurts and unhealed wounds don't vanish because a few words have been spoken but stay with us in the now we are living in.

It sounds pretty dismal, I know. It sounds as though most couples are doomed to stand by helplessly and watch as the bad feelings grow to such monstrous proportions that the love is choked off and withers away. Very often this is just what happens. But it doesn't have to be that way. Not if each embraces the other's anger as something that is as much a part of the relationship as love itself. Or, in other words, not if they can stop hating their anger and start loving it, at least accepting it.

If you can say to yourself and your partner, and really mean it, "I know that we are each entitled to our anger and that we will actually diminish and destroy the relationship we have if we don't acknowledge individual anger rights," then you can put anger in its proper place.

Considering the frustrations we all run up against every single day, most of us do a remarkable job of coping. Think about it. I don't know what your particular problems are, but if your life is anything at all like mine, you have to deal with washing machines and TV sets and cars that go on the blink (usually just when you need them most), mortgage payments, soaring medical bills, unwanted social and family obligations, job pressures and disappointments, not to mention traffic jams, long lines at the bank and supermarket, fuel shortages, the higher price of food, inflation, worry about the environment and aerosol sprays that deplete the atmosphere's ozone layer. And with all this, we continue to feel we have to put on a happy, cheerful life-is-just-a-bowl-of-cherries act for our spouses or lovers, day after day, night after night.

What rot. We're all entitled to establish our puny protests against our own personal inequities (indeed, if we don't, we may find ourselves in *real* trouble). Sometimes we rise above them. Sometimes not. Accept. Sometimes we strike out bravely, with courage and good cheer. Other times we slink home again, beaten. Accept. Accept it in yourself and in your partner. The two of you are close and the impact of your anger, even when it's not meant for one another, will shake you both. Accept. The anger you direct at one another will shake you even harder. But acceptance lends toughness and resiliency and you'll bounce back and your relationship will be all the stronger for what you've experienced together. The trick is to be aware of your anger, your suffering anger at the injustices of life itself *and* the anger you feel toward one another, and to know it's not bad, it's healthy and it means you're alive.

What you do with that anger depends on the kind of person you are and what's appropriate to the situation. A controlled tantrum may work on Monday, a retreat to your room on Tuesday, angry sex on Wednesday, and so on. If you can just keep releasing anger in small doses as it arises, you'll be okay. It's when you bottle up too much of it for too long that it gets you and the relationship into trouble.

Janie, a woman of twenty-seven, married only three years, told me that she had never shared negative feelings with her husband. "I wanted everything to be happy and good for us," she said. "I didn't want to spoil the time we spent together with nagging or complaining. But it didn't work. We had less and less sex and the relationship kept on getting deader and deader. One day he told me the marriage wasn't what he wanted after all. He didn't feel close to me anymore. I begged him to talk to me, listen to me, but he wouldn't. 'Too late.' That's what he said."

She told me that he turned to walk out of the room, and as he did, she grabbed at him. All she could get hold of was his shirt, which ripped as he pulled away.

"I hope I never have that feeling again," she said. "My hands were shaking. I wanted to kill him. My thoughts were so ugly and violent that I frightened myself. I still can't get over this terrible sense of being cheated. I had tried so hard. For three years I was pleasant and calm and understanding. And look what it got me . . ."

If Janie had been more realistic from the day of her marriage, and not expected a perfect "happiness," devoid of all "negative" but very natural human feelings, the relationship would not have reached an impasse.

Max, a forty-five-year-old lawyer, said that for twenty years he had been the recipient of his wife's anger, while he always held back, never ever giving her any of his own. A demanding woman who wanted more materially, emotionally, and sexually than he was able to give, she constantly attacked him with words and on several occasions slapped him or beat him with her fists. One day, he exploded, shouted obscenities at her and jumped into the car. Her response was to stand in the garage in front of the car, blocking him from driving away.

"I put the key in the ignition," he said, "and I swear I would have run her down if she hadn't stepped out of the way in time. I'm still thanking God that she did."

Janie and Max were casualties of their own anger. Janie felt like killing her husband and Max very nearly did kill his wife and all because of an accumulation of unresolved bad feeling. Perhaps if they had tried to deal with their anger, incident by incident, instead of saving it up until it became an emotional heap, their respective marriages wouldn't have collapsed. Or perhaps their marriages would have ended anyway, but Janie at least wouldn't feel so "cheated" and Max wouldn't be tormenting himself for the crime he almost committed.

If anger is part of every single one of us, it is part of every single relationship. When you have a real visceral understanding of this concept, anger ceases to be so frightening or so "bad," and becomes just another decent, normal, honest emotion. If you can accept this, you can stop battling with your anger (though not necessarily with one another) and start using some of that energy to get more of what you want out of your life and the relationship.

The happiest couples I've known are the ones who live with their anger just as much as they live with their love. They may fight a little or a lot. Some say they hardly ever "fight," but they disagree often and spend numerous hours working out their differences in spirited anger-talk. Others always seem to have their dukes up, but though the battles are real enough, a keen observer nevertheless detects an element of . . . well . . . "play" in them. Still others give one another the silent treatment, but not for long, and the silence is less a punishment than a signal.

It's important to be able to pick up on one another's anger signals, the little things your partner says and does that indicate a storm is coming. You know yourself that when you're angry, you want that other person to *know* it, even if you don't feel like coming right out and saying so. Your partner feels the same way. Once you've learned to recognize those signals (the portraits drawn on the various anger-types in this book may help), treat them with respect, which means *acknowledge* them; let your partner know that *you* know something's wrong. This shows you're concerned, and that even though you think he/she is overreacting or in the wrong, you care. Not to react at all is to indicate you really don't give a damn how your partner feels and it's all downhill from there.

Dave and Debbie, a young couple I know, have worked out, without ever having sat down to discuss it, a kind of nonverbal anger ritual. "When Debbie's angry, she clams up," says Dave. "Usually, I'm not aware that anything's wrong until I notice she hasn't spoken for a while, and then I take a good look at her and sure enough, she's wearing her 'mad face.' Well, that's when I do some heavy thinking. What happened? What went wrong? I know Deb so well now that I can usually figure it out myself. If I feel I've done something wrong, I go over and apologize. If I think she's wrong, I say so." He grins. "And maybe I'll throw in an apology anyway just for good measure. After that, she's quiet for a while. Thinking it over.

Then she'll come in all smiles and I'll know everything's okay. End of incident."

According to Dave, Debbie is just as sensitive to *his* anger signals and just as quick to respond, and this is one reason they're able to deal with their mutual angers so well.

Also, though they demonstrate great respect for one another's feelings, Dave and Debbie don't take themselves or their anger *too* seriously. Life is filled with frustrations which can and do get us down, but major tragedies are rare. They know this and they've learned to laugh at themselves and their ongoing domestic comedy of errors, petty annoyances, and hurt feelings. In a sense, they actually have fun with their anger. Anger as fun, or entertainment, is a novel idea for most people, but it's an attitude well worth cultivating. Do it, if you can. (Humphrey Bogart and his third wife Mayo Methot seem to have had this attitude. Some of their more spectacular battles were chronicled in an article in the *Atlantic* not too long ago, and their fighting was horrendous. He slugged her and she threw potted plants and whole roast turkeys at him. They were known as "the Battling Bogarts," and at one point they were barred as a couple from the "21" Club, though either was welcome alone or with friends. That the fighting was somehow "enjoyable" and an integral part of their being together came through in the article, and the author says there were "occasional signs that they even took pride in these fights.")

Another thing I've noticed about happy couples is the absence of any sexist myths about anger. Such as:

Anger is stronger in men than in women,
or Anger is stronger in women than in men,

and No real man ever gets angry at a woman,
or No real woman ever gets angry at a man.

If you've been laboring under any of these
myths, knock it (them) out of your head right
now. They have absolutely no basis in reality and
only get in the way of your granting one another
full anger-rights.

Some frigidity and impotence have been
directly traced to deep anger at a spouse. The
"proof" of this statement was dramatically illus-
trated in a recent divorce. The couple had been
married for twenty-five years, and during all that
time the man had accepted his impotence. Two
months after the couple's separation, the same
man was no longer impotent in a new relationship. At forty-eight he said happily, "I can be me,
in bed and out."

Accepting your mate's anger is at the very heart
of the matter. But if you haven't already given
yourself permission to feel angry, it's not easy to
allow for the emotion in someone else. With this
in mind, and assuming you're already clear about
your own anger rights (or are in the process of getting there), you might want to try some of the following anger exercises for couples.

Are You Part of a Sexed-Up Angry Couple?

1. Keep a week-long record of your anger. Include all the big and little things your partner
said and did that provoked your anger. Make a
note of how you handled each incident. Ask your
partner to do the same. At the end of the week, sit
down together and compare lists. Discuss the way
each episode was handled. What do you *wish* had
happened each time? Is there a pattern to your an-

ger? Are there two or three things that *always* set one or both of you off? Is anyone willing to change? If so, why? If not, why not?

2. Compare anger signals. Tell your partner how you know when he/she is angry. Ask your partner to tell you how he/she knows when *you're* angry. Have you each interpreted the other's anger signals correctly? Or do you have your signals crossed?

3. Next time you're angry, suggest going to bed. Afterward, ask one another whether the sex was better, the same, or worse. Did the sex have any effect on the anger? (Are you *still* angry? Talk about it. Is your anger gone? Tell each other about it.)

4. Switch roles. In a calm moment, stage a mock angry scene, with each of you acting the part of the other. See how well you can duplicate your partner's body language, facial gestures, speech, and mannerisms. Afterward, discuss your performances. What did you learn?

The Stuffer

"Anger? If I think I might be getting angry, I say to myself 'Keep calm,' and I try to focus on something else, something pleasant."

An Aware Stuffer

". . . If I *think* I *might* be getting angry . . ." Interesting. The statement above was made by a Stuffer, a person who has pushed his anger down so far for so long that he's not even sure what it *feels* like anymore.

Some Stuffers know when they are angry, all

right. But the idea of doing something about it, expressing it in some way, any way, is so frightening in terms of the way others might respond, that despite their seething insides, they mask their feelings, usually by adopting a grin-and-bear-it "what do I care?" attitude.

The route to stufferdom is almost always the same. As children these people are rather extravagantly rewarded for their goodness, sweetness, compliancy, and willingness to cooperate. At the same time, any questioning on their part, any honest statements about their own needs and wants, any demands, and, yes, any expressions of anger are either ignored or squelched, sometimes by severe reprimands and/or actual physical punishment.

So, the Stuffer usually gets the message early: his feelings don't count. Expressing them either gets him nowhere, or worse, gets him into trouble.

An articulate young man of twenty-seven, a writer I'll call Richard, confided that he had learned as a child that he had "absolutely no right to express any negative feelings."

He observed, "My mother used to drag me around with her all the time. When she visited her women friends, when she went to the supermarket or the beauty parlor, even when she went out to get a new bra or girdle. I hated it. It was boring. A kid in a lingerie store. What a mind-numbing experience. But heaven help me if I put up any kind of a fuss.

"To top it off, she was also a teacher at my school, so it seemed like she was always around, always hovering someplace in the background. I had no privacy. I couldn't have any secrets.

"My father? I didn't see as much of him as I saw of her. But they were alike. I got the same vibes from them both: be good, be nice, do as you're told, don't ask questions, don't talk back. *Or else*.

"When I was nice, they gloated and fussed over me. I was their 'angel,' their perfect little gentleman. When I acted up ... well ... I never got hit or anything, but I knew just where I stood. I'd fallen from grace.

"So I tried to be what they wanted: a good boy who didn't give any trouble. Another kid might have reacted differently, but I felt I had no choice. I just shut myself down, closed up like a factory that's gone out of business.

"All the while, deep down, *I* knew that if *they* knew what was really going on inside me, they'd freak out; their good boy wasn't such a good boy after all. But I went through my childhood wearing this 'good boy' disguise.

"I was a shy kid, afraid to try anything new because it might get me into trouble.

"I grew into my disguise. It began to fit so well that after a while I didn't know where 'good-boy Richard' left off and 'Richard the Kid,' the real Richard, began.

"I'm beginning to find out now, but I still have trouble expressing anger."

Like Richard, many Stuffers learn their lessons early and well: the way to get along in the world, the way to get love and approval, is to be agreeable and "nice." To disagree, to be assertive, even a little bit, to express anger, all are bad because they're dangerous. There's always the possibility (or so it seems to the Stuffers of the world) that people, originally Mom and Dad, but later on others, employers, friends, neighbors, lovers, their own children, and so on down the line, won't like them anymore. So they stifle, stuff, a lot of what might make them more effective, fully functioning human beings.

Stuffing, obviously, is a protective mechanism. People who stuff operate on the unconscious assumption that if they don't get angry at you, you won't get angry at them. There's no possibility of retaliation. No tit for tat.

The Unaware Stuffer

Richard is, or was up until recently, a Stuffer who didn't even know he stuffed. He'd done such a fine job of wrapping his emotions into a tight little bundle and then stuffing them down somewhere out of sight, out of mind, that he was no longer aware of the bundle and its dangerous contents. He had lost the ability to identify the vague sense of unease and disquiet he frequently experienced, the feeling that somehow something was *wrong,* for what it really was: anger.

In a sense, this kind of Stuffer is an emotional prude. Feelings of anger are not only dangerous but also bad, *indecent,* and they're blocked off in much the same way that people in the past censored their sexual feelings.

The Conscious Stuffer

The other kind of Stuffer, mentioned earlier, knows exactly what that ugly churning in his stomach is all about. He's conscious of angry feeling. But his awareness doesn't help much. He can't unstuff either. It's too scary.

How to Spot a Stuffer When You See One

Since they want love and approval so much, and since their way of winning and keeping it is to make sure they never ruffle *your* feelings, Stuffers can be very nice people to have around.

True, the Stuffer doesn't offer much in the way of intellectual stimulation because he's wary of conflict and won't risk angering you by expressing opinions and/or ideas that differ much from your own.

Still, Stuffers aim to please, so they're inclined to be "thoughtful" as well as agreeable. When your Stuffer friend bakes cookies, some of them will be set aside for you. If you happen to mention that you forgot to return your library books, you can count on the Stuffer to offer to drop them off for you.

Stuffers laugh and smile a lot.

They accentuate the positive. Though I've never known a Stuffer who actually came right out and *said* it, they operate according to the old adage that advises "If you can't say anything nice about a person, don't say anything at all."

Some Stuffers are not so much "nice" as they are cool. Nothing ever fazes them. They give the impression that they're in complete control of themselves in any and all situations, and whenever I see one of these people I can't help but be awed at the thought of all the psychic energy they can muster in order to keep their cool.

Cool Stuffers are sometimes admired, sometimes envied, and once in a while their very unflapability arouses one's anger. (As in, "I'd do anything to get a rise out of him/her.")

To be sure, there are times when keeping cool has its merits and may be the best way of handling a difficult situation. (More about this later.) But stuffing as a way of life is as unproductive and unhealthy for a person as going around blowing one's stack at every real or imagined slight.

Stuffers sometimes, though of course not always, run to fat. It's almost as though stuffing food helps them keep their anger stuffed.

Dorothy comes to mind. She's thirty-four, has close-cropped dark hair, a pretty face that seems always to be set in a pleasant, half-smiling expression, and an enormous body. *How* enormous I've never been able to tell because she always wears baggy pants topped by an even baggier sweater. Dorothy is married, and she and her husband appear to be a reasonably happy couple.

I asked Dorothy to fill out one of my anger questionnaires, and when two weeks had passed and I still hadn't heard from her, I phoned.

"I didn't know the questions were about anger," she said. Her voice, normally soft and with a lilting quality, had a strident, defensive note I'd never heard before.

"I never think about anger. It's disturbing to me. I'm afraid I just can't fill out your questionnaire."

Dorothy panics at the very thought of anger, both hers and anyone else's. She suppresses her own anger with food, literally stuffing, stuffing it down. It's her way of controlling the emotion, keeping it hidden. Except that her anger is there for all the world to see, in the ballooning layers of fat on her hips, her thighs, on her entire body.

I might add that Dorothy enjoys feeding others, too, and when you dine at her house you dine well. I've often heard her comment, "It makes me feel good to see people eat." Perhaps she hopes that in stuffing her friends, they, too, will stuff their anger?

Dorothy doesn't like being fat, but she's given up on trying to lose weight because she can't stay on a diet. But then how could she, when the need to stuff herself with food is so powerfully tied in with her desperate need to stuff her anger?

It seems obvious that before Dorothy can stop gorging and start losing weight, she'll have to accept the fact that she *is* angry, at least part of the time, and that her anger is a valid, valuable part of herself. In other words, she must learn how to unstuff.

Are You a Stuffer?

You and all the other Stuffers stuff at least partly because you fear the consequences of your anger (as well as its underlying causes). Perhaps you're afraid of retaliation and, what amounts to the same thing, loss of love and approval, which is partially what your anger is about in the first place. If you are, there's a good exercise, one I've recommended to Richard and Dorothy and other Stuffers I've known. It's called the Worst Thing That Could Possibly Happen Game.

1. To play it, one simply imagines the worst thing that could possibly happen as a result of verbalizing one's anger.

For example: suppose you're disappointed and unhappy (translation: angry) that someone else in your office got the promotion you were counting on for yourself. Now, imagine going and telling the boss how you feel about it. What's the worst thing that could possibly happen?

Well, if your boss is the kind who resents having to explain himself to his employees, you *might* lose your job. (Which could be a blessing in disguise, since an employer who feels he owes nothing but a weekly paycheck to the competent people who work for him is probably not a particularly good boss in the first place and you may be better off elsewhere.)

More likely, though, he'll explain why he made this particular decision. (He may even express surprise that you *wanted* the promotion, since as a Stuffer you may never have indicated any real desire to get ahead beyond doing your job in a conscientious way.) And once he's been made aware of your feelings, he'll probably be more apt to consider you for the next promotion.

The point of this game is to get you to open yourself up on all occasions. Certainly, in many situations you'll decide that stuffing is indeed the best policy. But in others, you may feel that stuffing is not in your best interests, although you'll stuff anyway, just to be on the safe side. Hopefully, there'll come a time when you'll decide you owe it to yourself to say what's on your mind and you'll say it and discover that, wonder of wonders, the world doesn't come crashing down around your feet as a result of expressing your anger, and that, on the contrary, expressing your anger can be an exhilarating, liberating experience.

2. Another kind of stuffing has to do with the fear of losing control. Many Stuffers suppress their anger not only because they're afraid of retaliation, but also because they suspect that if they ever do own up to their anger, they'll lose control, do

something violent, wreak some horrible, irreparable damage. The fear of losing control sometimes mounts to panic proportions.

When you feel the panic begin to rise, don't even try to stuff it; the cost in terms of your own psychic and physical health is far too dear. Instead, keep in mind that in a highly charged emotional state your body is prepared, indeed cries out, for *action*. So get moving and ride *with* the panic. Punch a punching bag. Run around the block three times. Mow the lawn. Clean out the garage.

When the panic subsides, and it will, it will, play the Worst Thing That Could Possibly Happen Game and decide whether or not you'll benefit by expressing your anger more directly.

Anger Between the Two of You

Hopefully, if you've read this far, you know at least a little bit more about your own anger.

You may have dredged up some anger while reading that you didn't even know you had before now (which is not bad, but good, very good, indeed; the anger was there all along, but now you know about it and you can begin to deal with it). You may have discovered that you're in an anger rut, and whether you stay in it or not, at least you know now that just because you've always done it "this way" doesn't mean you can't decide to do it "that way." You may even have learned to stop hating your anger, and if you have, it follows that you've learned to love yourself more.

Up to now, we've considered only one side of the anger story: your side. But there's another side, the one that belongs to the other people in your life. Some of them may have anger they don't even know about. Some of them may be in an anger rut. Some of them may hate their anger so much that their bad feelings about themselves prevent them from feeling good about anyone else. (Including you.) In any event, your anger affects them, their anger affects you.

Everyone knows that anger and the way it's expressed can ruin a marriage, a love affair, a friendship, a parental relationship, a career or just about anything else one values. But most of us are so down on anger that we never consider the possibility that it can also bring us closer to other people and actually enhance our relationships with them. Either way, it depends on how we react to one another's anger.

Just as you have options about the way you handle your own anger, you also have options for dealing with the anger that is aimed at you. Exercising those options is the key to coping with anger in others.

Before we go on, though, I want to emphasize that I'm *not* suggesting that you always follow the other person's lead, or that you automatically key all your reactions to the way the other person expresses anger. Far from it. If you did that, you'd lose yourself because you'd be running your life according to how other people feel and think.

I am suggesting that you can learn to respond according to what *you* want to happen in your relationships with those others. If there's love, and you want to keep that love flowing back and forth between you, there are ways to be angry without killing the good feelings. If there's ambivalence, you can use your anger to clarify and define the relationship. If there's alienation, anger can bring you closer, or deepen the rift, depending on how you choose to deal with it.

For most of us, the most disturbing of all angers are the chronic exchanges that take place between us and the people to whom we're closest, our spouses, our lovers, our children, our parents. Except for lovers, who may come and go with greater frequency than the others, these are the more or less "fixed" or "stationary" people in our lives. There is a constant interaction between us and them, if we're lucky, most of it pleasant, or at least not *un*pleasant. But no matter how much we may love these other people, and they us, that constant interaction causes friction. This is a simple fact, neither good nor bad.

Some people are troubled by the idea that most of their relationships are "flawed" by occasional angry feelings and that therefore these relationships aren't "good" (or not as good as they should be). If you go by this kind of reasoning, the "best" relationships would be the ones where there was never any friction because both parties were always gracious and smiling and bending over backward in order to be nice and accommodating to one another, and as a result, neither ever gets to know the "real" other very well. These "best" relationships would hardly qualify as relationships at all.

There can't be anything like true warmth and intimacy without anger coming into the picture, too. If you doubt this, think for a moment about the people you feel closest to. Aren't these the same people you feel most at ease with, most comfortable, most yourself? Aren't they the ones from whom you feel you have nothing (or very little) to hide, the ones who accept you wholly, not only when you're up and feeling good but also when you're down and blue and out of sorts? And angry?

The point, of course, is that feelings of closeness flourish where there is trust and acceptance of one's *whole* self. And since anger is part of each and every one of us, to love someone is also to accept his/her anger.

The last thing in the world that I want to imply, however, is that accepting someone else's anger means always turning the other cheek, or otherwise offering oneself up in the role of willing victim. What it does mean is granting full anger rights to the other person and recognizing that he or she is entitled to expressions of "negative" feeling. (This may be hard to do when you're still ambivalent about your own anger rights and your own freedom of expression. But in a sense, accepting yourself and accepting others go hand in hand, and as you make headway in one, you'll probably progress in the other.)

The more you know about someone else's anger, the better able you'll be to accept it and deal with it. If you're presently having big problems with someone you're close to, go through this book and see if you can identify their primary mode (s) of expressing anger. Better still, ask that person to look through with you.

Remember that many people are a combination of two or three related types and don't fit neatly into any one single category. No matter. You should have very little trouble making the identification (s) , and when you do, you'll not only have a better understanding of the hows and whys of that other person's behavior, you'll have a new basis for acceptance as well. It's easier, for example, to live with an Actor when you know those big scenes aren't staged for you and you alone, but are instead the Actor's generalized response to frustration; that it doesn't take much to set him or her off; that making a lot of noise and commotion relieves the Actor's tension; that the show usually doesn't last long and when it's over, it's over because the Actor rarely holds a grudge and may even feel a combination of dismay and remorse at the close of a scene. In the same way, if someone you're close to never loses his or her temper and hardly ever expresses negative emotion, you can suspect you're dealing with a Stuffer, in which case you'll understand that this person's perpetual and perhaps *maddening* (from your point of view) calm is a cover-up for great inner turmoil; that when he or she ignores *your* anger, it isn't necessarily out of cool control or a feeling of being above it all, but because anger itself is so terrifying to the Stuffer. (Certainly there are those rare, placid human beings who have a minimum of anger feelings in their makeup.)

Though I can't give you any sure-fire and specific behavioral "recipes" or "prescriptions" for using what you've learned, because no two individuals, even when they're of the same anger-type, can be expected to respond identically to an identical set of circumstances, a couple of examples may help you get a feeling for applying this information.

Let's say you're a Big Talker currently involved with a Stuffer. Anger is a no-no to the Stuffer as well as to most other anger-types who suppress any direct expression of the emotion (Body Person, Corner People, many Daydreamers and some Doers fall into this category). To be out of touch with one's true feelings or to have unrealistic fears about expressing them, as these people do, is unfortunate. But if you care about your Stuffer (or Body Person, or Corner Person, or whoever), try to accept those feelings about anger and also the way he/she deals with it. Does this mean you must give up "big talking" in deference to the Stuffer in your life? The answer is "No" (though one of the points I hoped to make in this book is that there is no one, good, all-purpose way of being angry and that people in an anger rut always benefit by trying to expand their repertoire of modes for expressing the emotion). Do all the "big talking" you like, but don't expect your Stuffer to respond in kind. He or she may indeed be feeling angry (or more probably "hurt"), but the Stuffer's way of handling it is to ignore it, or to perhaps withdraw from the room in a sulk. Either way, the behavior must be respected. Though *you* might feel better if your anger met with a *different* response, try not to feel cheated by the response you do get; it's the best the Stuffer can do. Your efforts to "get a rise" out of him or her will only make the Stuffer stuff harder.

What if the situation is reversed? What if you're the Stuffer and you're dealing with the Big Talker? If you've read the chapter on "big talking," you'll know that this person has a need to use words as a means of unloading angry energy that is as strong as your need to stuff. And just as hating yourself for stuffing is self-destructive, so is hating your Big Talker for talking destructively of the relationship. Chances are, the anger *you* feel (or pretend not to feel) is roughly equal to the Big Talker's and the difference lies in what you do with it. You may feel you get the worst part of the deal because you have to listen to all that noise, but the Big Talker wouldn't agree; he/she is frustrated by your lack of response.

Where do you go from here? Whether you're a Big Talker, a Stuffer, or any other anger-type, your options are clear: you can go on doing what you've always done (you may, in fact, be so locked into a particular pattern that you have no choice at the moment); or, based on what you've learned about the other person's anger, you can respond to it in ways that will decrease (or increase, if that's what you want) hostilities; or, you can encourage the other person to work *with* you toward an even deeper understanding of the anger that arises between the two of you. This last may be most difficult, but it also is potentially the most rewarding, and you will find that making the effort adds a whole new dimension to the relationship.

Assuming you've opted for the last alternative (you need no further information from me if you've chosen either of the first two courses), how do you proceed? I'm always wary of do's and don'ts (also, should's and shouldn'ts) and avoid them whenever possible, but a few of them seem to be in order here.

Cultivate an understanding that when someone else is angry at you, or you're angry at someone else, it doesn't mean that either of you has "failed," or that the relationship isn't a good one. It does mean that you've done or said, or in some instances "represent," something the other person doesn't like or perceives as a threat to his/her best interests, and that the other person feels comfortable enough in the relationship to *be* angry at you. (Many people, of course, are more hot-tempered or more sure of themselves and the way they think they deserve to be treated by others. For some of them, anger *always* feels right.

In a calm, cool moment when neither of you are angry, do sit down with the other person and trade anger "histories." Tell each other what you learned about anger as children. If you can't get the discussion off the ground, or it seems to be going nowhere, here are a few questions to ask one another.

When you were a child, how did your mother express anger at your father? How did your father express anger at your mother? Were their methods similar or different? What triggered their individual angers? And what was the reaction of each to the anger of the other? Would you say the *basic* feeling between them was one of warmth and caring? Disinterest? Disapproval? Hostility? What made you arrive at this conclusion?

Did your mother express anger at you? How? Did your father? How? In each case, what was most apt to trigger their anger? How did you respond to it?

Were you punished for being bad? How? As a child, did you feel you were being "justly" punished? As an adult, do you still feel the punishment was just? (or unjust?) What *was* considered "bad" in your family? As an adult, do you feel these same things are "bad?"

When you were little, did you feel loved? Merely tolerated? Disapproved of? What did your parents do (or not do) to make you feel that way?

What made *you* angry as a child? How did you express your feelings? Was your anger accepted? Ignored? Disapproved of? Do you see any similarity between the way you handled your anger when you were little and the way you handle it now? Do you see any similarity between the way either (or both) of your parents dealt with their anger and the way you now deal with yours?

Did you grow up with the feeling that anger was okay? Not okay? Very bad? How do you feel about it now?

This is a lot of ground to cover, maybe too much for one sitting. If you run out of time, or you find you're losing interest in the discussion,

by all means stop. But do plan to take up again
where you left off.

When two people take time out to ask each
other questions such as these, and when they answer thoughtfully and honestly, and when each
really concentrates on listening to the other, their
understanding of themselves and each other cannot help but be deepened.

That part about listening is enormously important, important enough to merit another "do." Do
listen conscientiously to what the other person has
to say.

Many people hear but do not listen when someone else talks; they recognize the sounds that
make up the words and the words that make up
the sentences and they may even nod to assure the
speaker that they're following his train of thought,
but they do not get the message. We all tune out
like this on occasion we can't/won't/don't give our
full attention to everyone all the time. Unfortunately, the people we're most likely to tune out
are the people with whom we interact most frequently, and thus, the very same people with
whom we may have the biggest, most troublesome
anger problems. By this I don't mean to imply
that anger is a function of not listening; in fact,
the reverse seems to be true; not listening is a
function of anger (see the section on "The Saboteur").

Real listening requires some effort, and a
special effort may be necessary when the speaker is
someone with whom you're frequently (perhaps
constantly) angry. But if you're really concerned
about that other person and want to do something
about your mutual anger problem, you can get
that feeling across by putting your own body at at-

tention. This means sitting slightly forward in your chair, facing the speaker. No fidgeting. Try to banish extraneous thoughts so that your mind will be open and receptive to what the other person says. It sometimes helps to try to look at that other person as though he or she were a brand-new friend. (Some people just can't manage to play this little game, however, and if you try it and find it hinders rather than helps your ability to concentrate, then give it up.)

In any event, do look at the speaker in addition to listening to the words and the tone of voice. You can also gain a lot of insight by noticing the body signals being transmitted. Are the lines of the body relaxed? Is he or she huddled in a self-protective, defensive posture? Or tensed as though ready for battle? Is the face animated? Or blank and impassive? A mask of sadness? Despair? Bitterness? Are the hands in repose? Do they flutter about nervously? Are the fists clenched?

Wonderful things begin to happen when people really listen to one another's anger. One of the best illustrations I know of involves a forty-year-old woman I'll call Doris, and her sixteen-year-old son, Tim. Doris told me that Tim had always been a sweet and loving child. As a little boy, he was docile and eager to please. "I couldn't praise him enough," Doris remembers. Then, at age sixteen, his behavior changed abruptly. He was alternately either sullen (a Stuffer) or given to temper tantrums (an Actor). Doris, of course, was bewildered. Her darling boy had turned, seemingly overnight, into an angry, sulking, name-calling, plate-throwing adolescent.

I suggested that she try to get Tim to sit down with her for a talk about anger. He resisted the idea at first. But she managed to get across to him that all she wanted was to know his feelings, and he finally agreed. Doris recounted their conversation in some detail:

"Tim told me that he's got to learn to be his own person, that he didn't want to be a mama's boy anymore, that the only way he could stop being one was to push me away. He just wanted me to leave him alone."

Doris realized then that anger was Tim's way of separating, of saying, "I'm growing up, I have to learn to stand on my own two feet." Her response was to tell him straightforwardly, adult-to-adult (because that's how Tim wanted it), that she understood more about his anger now, that she wouldn't stand for name-calling or for breaking property that belonged to her, but that she would try to respect his need for greater independence.

Tim apparently got the message, and though it wasn't completely smooth sailing from there on in, *he* knew how she felt and she knew how he felt and their relationship improved immeasurably.

Though anger information is the content of these little exchanges, caring and respect are the main messages. When you listen with your ears, your eyes, your head, your whole body, the other person is reassured. He or she has your attention. The need for screaming, calling names, breaking things, ostentatious sulking, etc., which are bids for attention as well as expressions of anger, is minimized. The sometimes desperate need to know that you care enough to listen and to want to share his/her feelings is satisfied.

One of the greatest anger-inducers is the feeling that someone doesn't give a damn (or that no one gives a damn). Conversely, one of the greatest anger-reducers is to indicate in words or in gestures that you *do* care, that you do want to understand.

Of course, no one can ever really know what goes on inside another human being and this is a terrible frustration both for the would-be understander and the one who wants to be understood, and we are all each of these, all the time.

The saddest truth of all is that each one of us *is* an island, locked into ourselves, we reach out blindly, sometimes gently and tentatively, sometimes violently, in an effort to get closer and to achieve oneness with others. Our efforts are doomed to failure, but we go on trying anyway. We try with our heads and with our bodies. We try with our love and affection and we even try with anger to get through to those others, to move toward them and out of our isolation. In a sense, then, anger is both a means to and a result of the closeness we crave so much.

Anger Exercises for the Two of You

The following exercises are for people who want to explore their anger together.

1. Take turns asking and answering the following questions:

How do you want me to respond to your anger?

Leave the room?

Watch silently?

Hold you?

Do what you do? (yell if you yell, sulk if you sulk, etc.)

Ask questions?

Other suggestions.

What joy do you get from your anger?

What part does anger play in our relationship? (Has it gone underground? Is it out in the open? Is there a lot of it? Just a little? Is it increasing? Decreasing?)

What happens between us that makes you most angry?

What do you feel when I get angry? (Hurt? Frightened? Angry? Numb?)

Who is the person in your life at whom you're most angry? Why?

2. Make a list of all the anger-types in this book, starting with the kind of anger most acceptable to you and ending with the kind least acceptable. Have your anger-partner do the same. Discuss your lists. Are they similar or very different? Why are certain anger-types more acceptable than others?

3. If you haven't already done so, identify your anger-type and have your partner identify his/hers. According to the lists you've made, are your anger-types "acceptable" to one another?

Anger Exercises for the Family

1. Have a family anger-session, children included, in which each member tells the way he/she feels about anger in relation to the others. Ask each other some of the questions listed in Exercise #1 of the previous section. If possible tape-record the session so that you can play it back in a few months or so.

2. The very next time one of your children cries (assuming the child is not physically hurt), ask why he or she is angry. You'll probably get an answer if the child is not afraid of you. Now is the

time to display an attitude of sympathy and acceptance (even though your feelings run to neither). Remember, the very young child feels powerless and has very little choice but to cry or scream or kick, or to say "I hate you, I wish you were dead." This may make you feel extremely uncomfortable and/or angry in return. But try to understand that the child is experiencing frustration and is entitled to react. Later on, you can impose limitations.

3. Encourage your older children to expand their anger repertoires. In a quiet moment, ask them about the last time they were angry and what they did about it. Discuss alternatives: What are some of the different ways they could have handled the situation? What are the pros and cons of each?

Anger in Other

Not-So-Close Relationships

Anger that arises between us and the people to whom we're closest is the most disturbing because we've made such an enormous emotional investment in these people. Somewhat less troublesome are the problems that crop up with the "peripheral" people in our lives, the ones we see from time to time or even every day, but with whom we have a less intense personal involvement. The less intimate of our friends, most neighbors, co-workers, teachers, students, and distant relatives fall into this category.

Probably you have neither the time nor the inclination for deep, meaningful anger-talks with each of them. Even so, there are a number of different things you can do to change the anger dynamics in any given situation.

An ongoing anger-exchange between you and one of these peripheral people deserves quite a lot of your attention. Many times, though certainly not always, the bad feelings are not a function of *that* relationship, but are carried over from some other, more intense relationship. Let me give you an example:

Isabelle, thirty-one, was an executive secretary for a large ad agency. She was very troubled by the enormous amount of tension that was building between herself and her boss. His voice had a certain "edge," a "bite," she told me, whenever he asked her to do something. However, she noticed it wasn't there when he spoke to the other employees. Isabelle freely admitted that she resented him and the way he "orders me around, and makes me feel pressured all the time."

I asked her how she responded to his requests. "I always do what he says," she answered, "because that's my job. But I let him know I don't like being pushed around. I yelled at him a few times, and once I spilled coffee all over his desk. I immediately realized it was a bad thing to do, so I covered up and pretended it was an accident. *I* knew it was deliberate, and I think *he* knew, too. Most of the time, when he asks me to do something, I just kind of fume inwardly. I don't know if it shows or not. It probably does."

On one occasion, I asked what being "bossed around" meant to Isabelle. I wondered if she could remember ever having been "bossed around" before. She thought about it a while, and then said, "No, it's the first time, not counting my father. My mother was sick and Dad wanted me to be responsible for the house. I hated it. I was a young teen-ager then and I wanted to be with my friends, but it was always, 'Isabelle, do this, Isabelle, do that, get me this, get me that . . .' "

As it turned out, though Isabelle really was angry at her boss for "pressuring her" as she put it, the feeling was triggered by an unhappy situation in her past. In a sense, her boss was a "stand-in" for her father, and his requests (which were in fact not unreasonable) were reminiscent of the demands her father made of her. Isabelle's reaction to her boss was a way of "getting even" with her father. The boss's response to Isabelle's testiness was inevitable: a reasonably good-natured man, he became churlish and overbearing in his dealings with her. Though Isabelle's new insight helped her to understand what was really happening between them, there was such a backlog of bad feeling that she finally decided to quit her job. However, she feels (and I do, too) that now that she knows the source of her anger, she'll be more able to separate her feelings about a future boss from the old anger she feels toward her father.

This kind of thing is not unusual. Under the right, or maybe we ought to say "wrong," circumstances, old, sometimes almost-forgotten anger from the past surfaces and is redirected at a new target. Much otherwise "unexplainable" anger can be explained this way.

Whenever you meet someone who, without actually doing anything that is openly hostile or offensive, "just seems to rub you the wrong way," sort through your memories. Ask yourself whether this person or the feeling you get from this person rings any familiar bells. If you can make a connection between the person, or feeling, and some past anger, then try to separate the old from new. Making connections with the past (especially if they hurt) is not easy, but you may be able to do it on your own without professional help. It's certainly worth a try.

What if *you* just happen to "rub someone the wrong way?" Unfortunately, there's probably not much you can do to get at the root of someone else's unexplained anger toward you. Unless he or she is in therapy or has read this book or is concerned enough about the situation to do some intensive do-it-yourself soul-searching, the anger is likely to continue unexplained.

Obviously, though, if you're very troubled or even just a little bit bothered by these bad feelings, you can always go directly to the other person and discuss the matter. He or she may deny being angry at first, in which case you'll have to decide whether to pursue it further. However, the very act of indicating your awareness and concern about what's happening will tend to modify the feelings between the two of you and may result in your seeing one another in a whole new light.

It is probably always a good idea to try to get at the source of anger that arises between you and one of these peripheral people, and since you're not a mind reader and neither is the other person, talking and listening are the only ways to do it. You can start off by asking such questions as:

1. Are you really angry at me or did something else trigger you?

2. How can we resolve this problem?

3. Are you feeling put down?

Once you've got the discussion going, listen, both to yourself and to what the other person has to say. Ask questions ("How?" "When?" "Why?" "What happened?" "How did you feel?") and invite him or her to do the same. Try to avoid phrases beginning with "You always . . ." "You never . . ." "You made me (do, say, feel, etc.) . . ." and words such as "fault" and "blame" (as in "It was all your fault," or "You were to blame for . . .").

When you're dealing with less than close friends or family, you're dealing with people you don't know very well. Obviously, much of their real selves are hidden from you (just as much of yours is hidden from them) simply because they don't feel close enough to reveal all. For this reason, a lot of the anger that arises between you and them may be caused by simple ignorance. You don't know, for example, how and when you might hurt their feelings, because you don't know what their feelings are in the first place. Which is all the more reason to at least make the effort to talk out your mutual angers.

In addition, it's always a good idea to privately monitor your own feelings and behavior. Is it possible that you actually enjoy making one of these people squirm? (And if so, why do you enjoy it?) Is it possible that they're angry as a result of your own callous or thoughtless treatment of them? (And if so, what do you get out of being thoughtless or callous?)

It's important to recognize that some tension inevitably exists whenever people have frequent dealings with one another. Bad vibes at the office can go on and on, and hidden "anger agendas" may be part of the everyday work routine. In the same way, neighborhood feuds can turn property lines into battle zones, with one side of the street literally not speaking to the other.

But it's also important to recognize that it doesn't have to be that way. Granted, anger is enormously powerful. But *your* anger is part of you. It *belongs* to you and you can direct it, deflect it, save it up, use it up, destroy with it, build with it, hate with it, love with it, and you can do all of these things some of the time and some of these things most of the time. The choice is yours.

Getting Out of Your Anger Rut

I am unalterably opposed to violence, war, and inflicting pain or suffering on any living thing, including oneself. Anger that achieves any of those ends is not only misused, it is hideous, ugly, destructive.

The Daydreamer, for example, may flail himself for drifting off into fantasy when things go wrong as opposed to doing something "constructive" with his anger. He may also feel guilty about the violence he puts into his fantasies. But the Daydreamer who envisions the destruction of the object of his anger doesn't enact that destruction, and is in a sense only one step removed from the fiction writer who takes those fantasies and puts them down on paper. Does the fiction writer feel guilty? I doubt it.

Daydreaming, in fact, is an excellent way of dealing with feelings—not the only good way to be sure, nor the best way under all circumstances. But if the daydreaming is held within reasonable bounds, if the fantasy doesn't overtake the reality of the situation, it's a fine technique for handling anger and many non-daydreamers would do well to adapt it. At appropriate times.

Telling your father-in-law you can't stand him probably won't get you much in real life except more anger in return and a family feud that no one wins, but you may be able to find some release in your imagination.

Now what about blaming? Anyone who is aware of being a chronic Blamer probably wants to do something different with his anger, at least some of the time. But is blaming always bad? What if the only way to save your own skin is to point the finger at someone else? For example, what if there's been a lot of tension at the office and your supervisor has been on your back all week and you're so angry at him that your mind is clouded and you make some stupid mistake that's going to cost the company a lot of money. The boss calls you in and asks for an explanation. By this time, you're even angrier at the supervisor and you would get great satisfaction out of blaming him for causing you to make the error. Could you? Should you? By blaming the supervisor, you'd get relief from your anger and his impatience truly did contribute to your mistake. In shouldering all the responsibility yourself, you might jeopardize your job, your anger is compounded, and the supervisor is off the hook. Take your choice.

Some children who are constantly being picked on by their parents become Blamers mainly in order to make their own lives more tolerable. Imagine poor Johnny who always gets slapped around for tracking mud through the kitchen. He's done it again, but Alison and Robert are with him. He just can't take another beating, so he decides to put the blame on one of the others this time. Can you blame him? The point, of course, is that even blaming may have an occasional valid time and place in one's anger repertoire.

As for the miserable Stuffer, he suffers a lot because it's awfully hard always pretending to be one thing (not angry) when what you really are is something else again (angry). But then again, you may *have* to stuff from time to time. Especially if you're one of those people who have trouble daydreaming.

Ordinarily, in those situations where a more direct expression of anger is inappropriate or unwise, I'd recommend daydreaming as a way to drain off the tension. But some people tell me that they're simply no good at imagining. (All children possess this creative power, incidentally, but the culture places such a heavy emphasis on "logic" and "reality" that some lose the ability by the time they reach adulthood.) So, if daydreaming doesn't work, you may deliberately choose to be a Stuffer instead and simply grin your way through those situations about which nothing can be done.

Or how about the double technique of stuffing now and doing later? Of containing your anger until you get home (or otherwise away from the anger-provoking person) and then releasing it in some form of physical activity?

This is an excellent technique for those times when direct confrontation with the object of your anger is impossible or unwise, or when the frustration you feel is the result of a situation over which you have no control. I've used it myself. (I remember one time driving along a highway in an area unfamiliar to me and having to go thirty miles out of my way because the road signs were ambiguous and poorly placed. I was steaming mad, but because I was driving I stuffed my anger until I got to my destination. First thing I did on arrival was write a strongly worded letter of complaint to the highway department. Next, still fuming, I borrowed a bicycle and went for a half-hour ride up and down the area's hilly country lanes. I felt *much* better by the time I got back, but I mailed that letter anyway.)

Though the Doer who does nothing else with his anger might want to vary his routine (and he should; chronic Doers often use activity as a way to hide the *source* of their anger from themselves), the rest of us would undoubtedly be better off by "doing" at least some of the time. Doing—making things, cleaning things, exercising, engaging in a sport, playing an instrument—is "constructive" in the textbook sense of the word. In using the body, built-up anger-tension and energy are dissipated, and you feel better as a result. Anyone can be a Doer. It takes no talent or special athletic ability; cleaning the house or washing the car works just as well as a fast game of tennis.

Humor is still another way of unloading those tense, angry feelings. We don't all have the ability to be spontaneously clever or witty, but most of us can be sarcastic at will, or at least repeat a joke we've heard from someone else. Whether one chooses to resort to humor is something else again. The Comedian *may* be well loved if his remarks are relatively barbless. More often, he is resented, or even feared, depending on the temperature of his delivery and the degree of malice reflected in his jokes. In any event, the Comedian has his own special way of dealing with feelings of hostility, and this technique, too, is something the rest of us might want to try from time to time.

Unless you've achieved some emotional flexibility, you're still locked into your childhood pattern where your feelings are concerned. You do what you've always done, *automatically*, and regardless of whether the outcome of your actions (or inaction) is *good* for you. It's hard to be good to yourself and to get what you want out of life when you're locked into *any* kind of pattern, or rut, because your responses are always in accordance with that pattern, and what happened in the past, rather than with people and events in the here and now.

An anger rut robs you of the power to act the way you want to act and be the way you want to be—now. It can also make you sick—literally. It can sap your emotional strength and energy. And choke off warmth and good feelings by separating you from others. When you get out of your anger rut, you'll be on your way to living a fuller and more satisfying life.

First, all through this book I've been urging you to experiment with alternative ways of handling anger, and now you can start *thinking* about anger in different terms. Read the following statements out loud to really "feel" the meaning behind the words:

• I'm a person and I'm often frustrated. It follows that I'm often angry.

• I don't hate my anger because it's part of me and I don't hate myself.

• I know things can't always go the way I want them to, but that doesn't mean I don't get angry anyway.

• I'm most angry at the people I love best. If I didn't love them so much, I wouldn't be so angry.

• It's good to let other people know how I feel—even when I'm angry.

• There is no such thing as having no right to be angry; there are only better and worse ways of expressing it.

After you have done this, talk to your friends and family. Ask them for their personal definitions of anger and about the way they express it.

You'll see that other people respond in many ways to anger and that should make it easier for you to take your first step toward getting out of your anger rut.

Beyond Anger: Your Golden Vision

Simply by reading this book you have expanded your thinking about anger; hopefully you have also exercised your anger "muscles" by practicing many of the anger exercises; I also trust that you have increased respect for your anger and that you use it wisely when necessary, that you are no longer threatened by the anger of others, and that you respect their angry feelings as well. If all this is true for you, you understand how to get angry without feeling guilty.

Is that all there is to anger? Are you simply entitled to a new diploma for your wall, Master of My Anger? The diploma is yours; you are one step farther along the road to understanding and handling an emotion which, when misused, can and does wreck people's relationships; you have gone beyond what your mother and father taught you was the right and proper way to deal with anger.

But ... there is another step, which I call your Golden Vision. You may never reach it, or you may attain it only later in your life.

To illustrate this Golden Vision, I think of Walt Whitman, the famous American poet of whom it was said: "He was equipped with an emotional brain so harmonized and balanced that it simply did not generate those poisons which spoil the lives of others not so gifted."

A disciple of Whitman's (Dr. R. Bucke) reputedly commented: "When I first knew him, I used to think that he watched himself, and would not allow his tongue to give expression to fretfulness, antipathy, complaint . . . It did not occur to me as possible that these mental states could be absent in him. (In terms of this book, Bucke thought that Whitman was a Stuffer, but the difference between stuffing your anger and actually no longer feeling it is vast.)

So the golden vision of you as a person is to go beyond your anger to where you are indeed immune at the core to this emotion.

However, it is a vision that will never work until you have taken all the steps necessary to observe and understand and face your angry feelings as they are . . . this very day. You cannot omit steps in the process of becoming a less angry "you." You cannot pretend you are someone that you are not. Then you succumb to being a Body Person, a Stuffer, a Corner Person.

It is only through digging at your anger, looking at it squarely, that you get even a chance at the Golden Vision.

If you know one person whose sense of joy is so expansive, so contagious, so bright in its dazzling radiance, you have a model for your vision. And when you see a person like that, there is no mistaking that person for a Stuffer.

This kind of human being was either not overladen with heavy prohibitions against anger in childhood, or has himself managed to emerge from the anger as truly joyous.

Somewhere in your thoughts as you wrestle and wonder and fight and acknowledge your angry feelings and those of others and make up and begin your anger all over again, imagine that these heightened feelings are possible for you to experience, that you can truly be at oneness with yourself, others, the universe.

This experience is possible no matter how bleak the external world may be, no matter what very real problems you may face each and every day. This kind of person is wholly human, and it is certainly a vision worth working for.

Good luck! And good work!

Appendix

Sample Questionnaires

I would appreciate your answering the following questions about ANGER. Please be as frank and honest as you can (I'm not asking for your name, it's your feelings I'm after).

1. Complete this sentence: Anger is   *caused by frustration.*

2. What did you learn about anger as a child?
Since there was a lot of silence in my home as a child, and anger the only emotion, arguments and physical violence became abhorrent to me. Not wishing to be like my parents, I held my anger in. Feeling anger and witnessing someone else's anger frightens me.

3. How did you express your anger as a child?
Since I didn't want to feel angry, I usually felt the uselessness of a situation and got depressed, disappointed. I do remember a few times, not during specific angry periods, probably just frustration periods, when I would just want to punch something. My sister obliged me, as if it were a game, and held a pillow for me to beat up on.

4. Describe your most recent "anger" experience?
I got angry at a friend who I thought was taking advantage of me. We didn't discuss the situation, and I'm sure he didn't even know I was mad. The incident reoccurred and still nothing was said. I realized my friend was not a mind reader, and that either I had to tell him how I felt or forget it. Very soon my anger disappeared.

5. Describe the most angry moment in your entire life.
When I was ten or eleven years old, I had a collection of china and porcelain horses which meant a great deal to me. My sweet sister asked me one day what I would do if she were to jiggle the table they were on and break them. I told her I would probably hit her. She jiggled the table

and all of them smashed. I didn't do anything except cry,
and thought I would never forget, or forgive her.

6. List the varieties of ways in which you deal with
anger.

I haven't changed much in dealing with anger. I still
hold things inside. I've tried writing as a release. I would
write the most terrible letters to people and, of course,
never mailed them. Later, upon rereading them, it was al-
most uncomprehensible that I could feel so hateful and
unjust.

7. What pleasure do you get from anger? *Absolutely*
none.

8. Do you have any positive way of getting rid of anger?
If so, how?

Experience has shown me that if I dwell on an anger-
producing incident, I upset myself uselessly. So I give the
situation time, a day or so, and it clears itself up.

9. How do you use anger as a weapon against others?

Toward the opposite sex, my silence has always seemed
like a form of torture. I don't use it purposely, just by
force of habit. It's a terrible habit—silence.

10. What is your definition of anger?

Very difficult to define, it's such a gnawing, twisting
feeling, a self-defeating emotion.

11. What is your definition of hostility?

Insecure unfriendliness.

12. What is your definition of aggression?

Someone unafraid to step on toes to get ahead—for
selfish reasons.

13. What do you find are "special anger problems" in
the male-female relationship?

Being uncommunicative causes anger-misunderstandings.

Here is a sample questionnaire to be filled out by you.

1. Complete this sentence: Anger is

2. What did you learn about anger as a child?

3. How did you express anger as a child?

4. Describe your most recent "anger" experience.

5. Describe the most angry moment in your entire life.

6. List the varieties of ways in which you deal with anger.

7. What pleasure do you get from anger?

8. Do you have any positive way of getting rid of anger? If so, how?

9. How do you use anger as a weapon against others?

10. What is your definition of anger?

11. What is your definition of hostility?

12. What is your definition of aggression?

13. What do you find are "special anger problems" in the male-female relationship?

Suggestions For Further Reading

Bach, Dr. George R., and Goldberg, Dr. Herb, *Creative Aggression*. Garden City, New York: Doubleday & Company, Inc., 1974.

Chesler, Phyllis, *Women and Madness*. Garden City, New York: Doubleday & Company, Inc., 1972.

DeRopp, Robert, *The Master Game*. New York: Dell Publishing Co., Inc., 1968.

Janov, Arthur, *The Primal Scream*. New York: G. P. Putnam's Sons, 1970.

Leboyer, Frederick, *Birth Without Violence*. New York: Alfred A. Knopf, 1975.

Lorenz, Konrad, *On Aggression*. New York: Harcourt, Brace Jovanovich, 1966.

Storr, Anthony, *Human Aggression*, New York: Bantam Books, Inc., 1970.

Weiss, Edward, and English, O. Spurgeon, *Psychosomatic Medicine*. Philadelphia: W. B. Saunders Company, 1949.

About the Author

Adelaide Bry is a psychotherapist who, in addition to conducting a clinical practice, runs frequent workshops in transactional analysis for business groups.

She is a frequent guest on Philadelphia area radio and television shows and has appeared nationally with Mike Douglas, Johnny Carson, and David Susskind.

In addition to HOW TO GET ANGRY WITHOUT FEELING GUILTY, New American Library has published Adelaide Bry's THE SEXUALLY AGGRESSIVE WOMAN, PRIMER OF BEHAVIORAL PSYCHOLOGY, and INSIDE PSYCHOTHERAPY.